IMAGES OF ENGLAND

SUNNY VALE PLEASURE GARDENS
'A POSTCARD FROM SUNNY BUNCES'

BARD OF AVON & PEACE LODGES
M.U., I.O.O.F., HALIFAX.

ANNUAL

SUMMER TREAT

On Saturday, July 9th, 1938,
— TO —

SUNNY VALE
HIPPERHOLME.

In addition to all the Popular Attractions and Amusements
of the Pleasure Park,

PUNCH and JUDY and SPECIAL ATTRACTIONS from 3 p.m.

MUSIC Relayed throughout the Grounds.

And for Boating, Open-Air Dancing and Skating.

**All Juveniles to ASSEMBLE at the Friendly and Trades
Societies' Club, St. James's Road, at 2 p.m.**

**SPECIAL BUSES will leave the Club prompt for
Sunny Vale, returning at 8 p.m.**

Adult Members and Friends—

Trains leave Halifax 1-58 & 2-48 for HIPPERHOLME.

Return Fare 3½d.   Return by any Train—7-53, 8-40, 9-24.

INCLUSIVE TICKETS for ADMISSION and SPECIAL TEA, with Sweets
(Extras: Meat, Fruit, Salmon, Salad, etc., may be had at the Tables),
ADULT MEMBERS & FRIENDS, 1/3.

Accommodation Reserved in Tea Rooms for all Ticket holders.

JUVENILE MEMBERS FREE.

All Children must assemble in front of Tea Rooms at 8 p.m. for return by Road.

Tickets may be had from the Secretaries—Mr. H. MALLALIEU, 14, Norman Street,
Fenton Road; Mr. S. HALLIDAY, 21, West Mount Street, Pellon Lane.

Juvenile Members must have Official Badges, which may be had from the above.

ENROL YOUR CHILDREN IN THE ABOVE SOCIETY.

ARE **YOU** GOING ?   IF NOT, WHY NOT ?

IMAGES OF ENGLAND

SUNNY VALE PLEASURE GARDENS

'A POSTCARD FROM SUNNY BUNCES'

CHRIS HELME

TEMPUS

Frontispiece: Within the first three years of its opening in 1880, originally as the Sunny Vale Pleasure Gardens, Sunny Vale had become a place for those late nineteenth-century mid-summer Sunday strollers to take in the country air. In the first three years it attracted over three hundred visitors from the local community. Nestling in the Walterclough Valley, situated between Hove Edge and Hipperholme on the outskirts of Halifax, in the old West Riding of Yorkshire, for many children Sunny Vale was to become the venue for their Annual Sunday School Summer Treat, the highlight of their year. This was a special place in the hearts and minds of many people for over three quarters of a century. To the countless numbers of children who visited and spent happy days there, it was simply known as Sunny Bunces. This local Independent Order of Odd Fellows advertisement illustrates just some aspects of what made it such a special place.

First published 2007

Tempus Publishing Limited
The Mill, Brimscombe Port,
Stroud, Gloucestershire, GL5 2QG
www.tempus-publishing.com

© Chris Helme, 2007

British Library Cataloguing in Publication Data.
A catalogue record for this book is available from the British Library.

ISBN 978 07524 4355 3

Typesetting and origination by Tempus Publishing Limited.
Printed in Great Britain.

Contents

Acknowledgements

Having been involved in local history for over thirty years, there have been many people throughout these years who have helped and encouraged me. For sharing their memories and photographs I will always be grateful. I am pleased to say that many of their photographs have been included in this publication.

I am sure the very thought of the Sunny Vale Pleasure Gardens will evoke memories from the childhoods of many readers. Over the last twenty years I have collected personal memories from countless people who visited Sunny Bunces, the name most visitors knew it by. In some cases these memories date back to before the First World War.

I am pleased to have had the opportunity of including many of those personal memories, in some cases from people who have since passed away. The treasured memories they brought to mind can now be shared and appreciated by us all.

These documented memories not only give a glimpse into their visit to Sunny Vale but an insight into aspects of the lives they led at the time. Whilst many of the photographs in this publication are from my own collection, there are a few others that have been kindly loaned by friends and contacts. In addition there are a number of other people who have contributed information and advice for this publication. I would like to take this opportunity of thanking them all.

These individuals include: Chris Freeman, Steve Gee, Dr Vanessa Toulmin, PhD National Fair Ground Archive Research Director, Mrs E. Woodhead (née Henley), Mrs D. Maude (née King), Ronald Helme, Gerald Hartley, John Brooke, Mike Hardcastle, Greta Imeson, Derek and Vera Hamer, Robert Brett, Paul Williams (Florida) for his Stock Car memories and Jean Vasey for the Stock Car programme information and Alan Scott for his Bradford theatre-world knowledge.

Copyright approval has been sought wherever it has applied but in certain cases copyright could not be traced; I would still like to thank all those unknown people.

And finally … I would like to give a special thanks to Mrs Lionne Crossley, the granddaughter of Joseph Bunce, Mr Gaston (Gab) and Mrs Rita Delorme, the current owners, for their support throughout my research and preparation work for this publication.

Introduction

I suppose the first time I heard about the Sunny Vale Pleasure Gardens would have been whilst visiting my grandparents' home in Hipperholme during the early 1950s. Grandma would tell me about her childhood days and would talk about a place that she described as being a 'truly magical place', hidden away in the Walterclough Valley. This valley I later discovered extended from Brookfoot between Brighouse and Elland up to the next valley at Shibden, near Halifax and skirted past Brighouse, Hove Edge and then Hipperholme.

Grandma was born in 1905 and was taken to Sunny Vale at first, like most of the other Hipperholme children, with the local Sunday school on their Annual Sunday School Treat. One of the many things she told me about 'Sunny Bunces', as she called it, was that when she was a young girl you could actually mail a postcard to a relative who lived locally in the morning and it would be delivered by the postman to their house the same day.

It was about 1961 before I was allowed to venture down into the valley with a few friends to try and find the place that Grandma spoke of. I recall finding the two lakes: a rather grim and unwelcoming kind of place, nothing like the place Grandma had described to me. However, my friends and I spent a few enjoyable although childish hours trying, be it unsuccessfully, to recover a submerged rowing boat from the smaller of the two lakes.

What had happened to the so-called 'truly magical place' that Grandma had told me about and why was it called 'Sunny Bunces'? According to stories from other older people it attracted as many as 100,000 visitors each year and that was before the 1920s. But what did they all come and see and what did they do once they were here?

Gradually, over a period of time and piecing together the story of what I now refer to as 'the playground of the North', has come a fascinating insight into the social changes which all began in 1880 when Mr Joseph Bunce and his new wife Sarah Jane Farnell moved into the Walterclough Valley.

I hope once having read this book, that for those who visited Sunny Vale it will bring back happy memories of a distant childhood and days of being young and carefree and that those readers who never visited Sunny Vale will marvel at exactly what they missed.

Enjoy…

Chris Helme

E-mail: enquiries@chrishelme-brighouse.org.uk

Donkey rides at Sunny Vale during the 1920s. Over the years I have presented a slide show on the history of Sunny Vale to audiences of every age group. By far the most difficult but equally inquisitive audiences and always refreshingly enthusiastic have been schoolchildren. Explaining to junior school children that there was a time when people would go to Sunny Vale as their annual holiday quite often prompts the question, 'did they stay in a hotel?' The concept of visiting Sunny Vale for just an afternoon – which for those children amounted to being the sum total of their annual holiday – comes as quite a shock. Looks of disbelief are not unusual from present-day schoolchildren who take visiting the different continents and staying in hotels as the general standard.

one

When It All Began

Try to imagine you are a small child of eight or nine years old and it is the early years of the twentieth century. You do not live near a river, a canal or even a mill dam and the nearest coastline is seventy-five miles away. So, what would be the largest expanse of water you as a child of that period would have seen? It is more than likely to have been no more than what I will describe as the 'mobile bathroom' – that is to say, the long tin bath which was hung on a nail at the back of the cellar door. That old bath would be dragged out on Friday nights, with each member of the family taking it in turns to have their weekly bath. Of course, it would be dad first and then it would gradually work its way down to the smallest and youngest member of your family – you. To instil a bit of decorum to this weekly event, for female members of the family, the clothes horse would be draped in sheets and then positioned strategically around the bath.

Now try to imagine being the same child visiting Sunny Vale Pleasure Gardens for the first time and being faced with two huge lakes and an almost endless number of beautifully painted rowing boats. That scene I am sure would remain etched in your memory forever, just as it did for all those children who visited the Sunny Vale Pleasure Gardens – somewhere that was often referred to as 'the playground of the North'. This Edwardian multi-view postcard illustrates what must for many children have been a truly remarkable experience.

Going to Sunny Bunces

I was born in September 1916. On my fifth birthday my mother and father took me to Sunny Vale, as a treat for my birthday. We caught a train to Hipperholme and then had a long walk down to the pleasure gardens. When we got there I stood in amazement, just staring at all the things I could see. I wanted to ride on the flying chair ride, but a man said I was too young. We made our way to the lake, where we could see rowing boats and a steamer, which went round the lake. I went on a rowing boat and thought it was wonderful. Going to Sunny Bunces, as we always called it, has been one of the lasting memories from my childhood.

Mrs Marian Corp (recorded memory 20 September 1990)

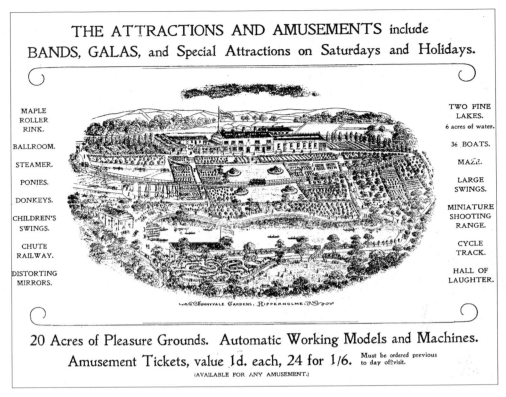

THE ATTRACTIONS AND AMUSEMENTS include BANDS, GALAS, and Special Attractions on Saturdays and Holidays.

MAPLE ROLLER RINK.

BALLROOM.

STEAMER.

PONIES.

DONKEYS.

CHILDREN'S SWINGS.

CHUTE RAILWAY.

DISTORTING MIRRORS.

TWO FINE LAKES.
6 acres of water.

36 BOATS.

MAZE.

LARGE SWINGS.

MINIATURE SHOOTING RANGE.

CYCLE TRACK.

HALL OF LAUGHTER.

SUNNYVALE GARDENS, HIPPERHOLME.

20 Acres of Pleasure Grounds. Automatic Working Models and Machines.
Amusement Tickets, value 1d. each, 24 for 1/6. Must be ordered previous to day of visit.
(AVAILABLE FOR ANY AMUSEMENT.)

This is another example of Sunny Vale's publicity material — it has been said that the same image was used originally as a transfer print on a wall of white ceramic titles in the tea rooms. As the visitors queued up for their pre-ordered tea of quartered sandwiches, a piece of cake, some crisps, a cup of tea or a glass of aerated water for the children they could all stare at it in amazement. Whilst this image was originally only an artist's impression of what Sunny Vale was to look like when it was finally complete, I am sure many older readers will identify and remember some of the amusements from when they visited as children.

A ride on the Scenic Air Chair

It was a sunny day in about 1928, when our choir from Royston Primitive Methodist church, South Yorkshire, went for a day trip in a charabanc. We went on a rowing boat on a lake; I seemed to be the only young person (thirteen years old) in the boat. I do remember there were two tenors rowing the boat and three sopranos along with me in as passengers. We went in a Maze and had a ride on a scenic air chair. We all went roller-skating and as I spent most of my time on my bottom, my white dress and knickers soon became pretty grubby — so much so that that was the last time I went roller-skating. I have memories of us all congregating in a large room to have sandwiches and tea. I also remember that my father, who was the choirmaster, was presented with a beautiful conducting baton. Funnily enough, I was recently in Manchester Airport collecting a cup of tea from a vending machine and a young man stood at the side of me commented 'these new inventions'. 'Not so…' I said, 'there were machines like these at Sunny Vale when I was a young girl.' Placing your money in a slot machine, you could get either a drink or a piece of cake from a stand that went round for you to choose which piece of cake you wanted. It was a long time ago.
Miss Doris Westerman (recorded memory 28 August 1990)

There will probably be some readers who are now still wondering just where this wonderful place was. Well, it was situated in the Walterclough Valley, which is almost a continuation of the well-known Shibden Valley and is situated between Brighouse and Halifax (Calderdale Metropolitan District Council) in what we now call West Yorkshire but in earlier days was part of the old West Riding. The valley took its name from Walterclough Hall, an ancient property that dated back to the sixteenth century but which was demolished many years ago.

On the Brighouse side of the valley (to the left of this view) was the Walterclough Pit, whilst on the Halifax side (to the right of this view) was Allen's Brickworks, a place that was of some importance to young female visitors in particular, which I will explain later. Over the hill on the opposite side of the valley to where this man is working in the fields is the small hilltop village of Southowram. Many of the local children from that community made their way down into the valley. This was to a place that became known as the alternative way of getting into Sunny Vale. This was a well-kept secret amongst the children of Southowram, a journey that generations of children would take, a route that showed them all how to sneak into Sunny Vale, without paying.

From left to right: Sarah Jane, Joseph and his sister. Many people find it surprising that Joseph Bunce was someone we often refer to as a 'comer-in' (someone not from these parts). He was the second son of James and Esther Bunce and was born in Totteridge in Hertfordshire in 1850.

He was educated at Totteridge Lane Chapel School, a local charity school. He was one of twelve boys who benefited from the charity by having their fees paid, being supplied with a corduroy suit and given a pair of new boots annually. Also included, courtesy of the Lord of the Manor, was a New Year's Day meal.

In 1868 he came to Yorkshire for the first time, working as a gardener in Wetherby. However, over the next six years he had a number of similar jobs throughout the North of England. In 1874 he moved to Halifax, working with his father at a market garden in the Wheatley area. In 1876 at Square Congregational chapel Halifax he married Sarah Jane Farnell. They were both Sunday school teachers, with Joseph eventually being appointed as superintendent.

On 1 May 1880, they moved to Lightcliffe Wood Bottom Farm, Hove Edge, taking on a two-acre smallholding known as Sunny Vale Nurseries with the intention of starting their own business in market gardening. During the summer months it was noticeable that many Sunday strollers from Hipperholme, Hove Edge, Southowram and Brighouse, including many Sunday school groups, would all pass by their home and would even stand outside exchanging news and gossip. This was whilst their children were making their own entertainment playing in the nearby fields.

As the number of people passing by gradually grew Sarah Bunce conceived the idea of providing some basic catering for them – with cups of tea, sandwiches and minerals for the children – and of course, charging them for this new service. Joseph increased the original two acres by taking on a further twenty acres and gradually over the next twenty-five years increased it to forty acres.

With the steady increase in the number of people visiting, which included even more families from further afield beginning to attend, a new name was becoming commonplace amongst the local community. When people would enquire where you were going on Sunday, the answer was 'Sunny Bunces' – a name that was soon to become a byword for fun, entertainment and a good time, something that was to continue for the next seventy-five years.

As the reputation of Sunny Vale grew, so too did that of Joseph Bunce himself within the community, so much so that he began to take a keen interest and greater role in local affairs. In 1896 he was elected to the Brighouse Borough Council as the representative for the Hove Edge Ward. Through his expertise as a gardener he served on the Parks and Cemeteries Committee.

In 1901 when tramcar transport was in its infancy he moved a resolution at a Brighouse Council meeting that Halifax be asked to extend their tramcar route from Stump Cross through to Hipperholme, down through Hove Edge with the terminus being in Brighouse town centre. Seen as a shrewd business move by his fellow councillors because the tramcars would have to pass the access roads to Sunny Vale, it was defeated because of the self-interest. However, the new tramcar route was completed in 1904. With transport now more readily available, Sunny Vale went from strength to strength. In October of 1908 he died at his family home, aged sixty-seven.

James Farnell Bunce was born in 1878 and was the elder of Joseph and Sarah's two sons. From an early age he helped his parents to convert their farm and market garden into what became the best inland resort in the North of England.

Hour after hour, day after day, he and other helpers brought load after load of stone down from the hillside into the valley bottom. This was to construct the foundations for many of Sunny Vale's future attractions. These were laid down so well that even up until comparatively modern times, years after the disappearance of the attractions themselves, many of the old foundations still survived beneath the undergrowth.

Even with all this activity the nurseries at Sunny Vale were in a healthy state and gardeners came from all over the West Riding. Joseph Bunce & Sons also became illumination specialists, and went on to successfully carry out large contracts for illuminations at Lister Park, Bradford, Low Moor, Greenhead Park and Huddersfield.

James, or 'Mr Jim' as he was known, married Florence Eva Lister and lived in one of the five cottages known as 'Bunces Row' – cottages which have long since been demolished.

This was really 'living on the job' in the truest sense, when all he had to do was walk out of the front door and nip over his garden wall into the grounds and his place of work. Sadly, Florence died on 20 March 1916, aged thirty-eight, leaving him to bring up their thirteen-year old daughter Amy. In 1919, James married Florence Mabel Greenstreet and they had a son, Joseph Peter, who was born in the following year and then a daughter, Lionne, in 1922.

Throughout his life James was always recognised as the 'doer' of the family, the man who kept things working at Sunny Vale. Many stories have been told about 'Mr Jim', who was often described as a 'sober sort of chap'.

In 1911 he became the new owner of what was originally called the Empire Theatre in Atlas Mill Road, Brighouse, premises which had been originally opened as a theatre. However, with the changing times it was converted into a skating rink in 1909 but this new craze did not last long. James decided to move with the times by showing silent films and then have skating sessions between the films.

Owing to a number of difficulties, the following year the ownership of the old Empire Theatre had changed and by 1918 had closed down completely and was demolished not long after. During the First World War James was gassed and had to be cared for at a Voluntary Aid Detachment (VAD) hospital in the South of England. This photograph shows James in his hospital uniform. The effects of the gassing remained with him for the rest of his life, though working outside throughout his life helped to relieve them. James worked at Sunny Vale until the family decided to sell it in 1946. He died on 23 April 1952, aged seventy-two.

George Percy Bunce was the youngest son of Joseph and Sarah Jane Bunce and was born in 1881, at the family home at Sunny Vale.

Like his brother he also spent many hours in those early days helping his father to create Sunny Vale and make it into what became known as the ideal holiday at home.

George married local girl Maria Mitchell, the daughter of Mr and Mrs Harry Mitchell of 'South View', Lightcliffe Road, Brighouse, whose family had been involved for many years with the Hipperholme Urban District Council. Probably with this in mind and the fact that his own father had been elected to the Brighouse Borough Council in 1896 as the Liberal candidate for the Hove Edge Ward, he too became deeply involved in public affairs.

He followed in his father's footsteps as the newly elected Liberal councillor for Hove Edge in 1923. In 1934 he became a Justice of the Peace and in 1939 became an Alderman of the Borough, a position he retained until his retirement from local politics in 1945.

His proudest achievement came on 9 November 1942 when he was appointed the Mayor of Brighouse, with Maria acting as his consort. They held this distinguished position for the then-customary two years. Throughout his public life he was often still to be found

working down at Sunny Vale, not unlike his brother, keeping everything in good working order but dealing with the countless bookings and the day-to-day business administrative matters involved in running such a successful enterprise. He died on 1 January 1948, aged sixty-seven.

On Special Occasions

I was born in Halifax in 1900 and well remember being taken to Sunny Bunces, as we knew it when we were children. It was in a wooded valley with a stream running through it. There were two lakes, used for boating, and there were swings and a helter-skelter where you sat on a mat and slid to the bottom. There were firework displays on Saturday evenings and on special occasions. It was very popular with young people and flourished while owned by a Mr Bunce. However, after he sold it, it fell into disrepair. I enjoyed many teenage happy hours there and in later years I even took my own children but it was not the same.

Mrs Doris Wilkinson – St Albans (recorded memory 9 August 1990)

KISSING IN SUNNY VALE GARDENS,
HIPPERHOLME.

Our Specialist recently visited Sunny Vale and the following observations may be taken as correct. He found that **Brighouse** girls keep quite still till they are well kissed and then say "I think you ought to be ashamed of yourself." An **Elland** Girl, when kissed, closes her eyes in ecstacy, and does not open them again until she is quite sure there is no more, The damsels of **Morley**, on being osculated, timidly suggest a "walk" **In the Garden**. The young ladies of **Sowerby Bridge** recognise the "rights of man," receive the chaste salute with meekness, and turn the other cheek. The charming young ladies of **Bradford**, when kissed, propose a visit to the **Swing Boats**. A **Dewsbury** girl only allows one kiss for every twelve laps round the **Dancing Rooms**. The girls of **Halifax** object to be under any obligation, and insist on giving as good as they get. After 47 kisses a **Slaithwaite** girl refuses to have more and returns those she has already had. When a **Shipley** girl is suddenly kissed she says "Oh" very softly, for fear someone should come and stop it. A marriagable maiden of **Huddersfield**, on being kissed, tries to look stern, fails, then slides her little hand into that of the bold, bad man, and in a voice as soft as Blance Mange, whispers tenderly, "Oh George, what are your intentions?" He also found that all the girls had a weakness for **Donkey Rides**, and the **Puzzle Gardens** are never missed as there are quite a lot of corners. After a couple are once started in the **Swing Boats** it is only the thoughts of tea that will bring them out.

N.B.—No kissing is permitted in the gardens on Sundays. Interest charged on all overdue accounts.

Visiting Wonderland

I first got to know Sunny Vale or Sunny Bunces as it was called by everyone living in Hove Edge, Hipperholme and Southowram – these are the little places round Sunny Vale. I came to live in Yorkshire from Derbyshire in 1935, at the age of seven years. When I went to it for the first time it was like wonderland. I came to live at the top of Half House Lane (Hove Edge) which led down into Sunny Vale. On the way down you passed Stead's fish and chip shop and Ripley's ice cream place, where they made the ice cream to sell in the pleasure park.

I went for my tea in the park for the Coronation of King George VI with St Chad's School; we all got a mug, I still have it in the house somewhere. Our tea was one teacake with icing on, one plain bun and one cream bun, a mug of tea and one shilling's worth of tickets to go on the rides. We got in free that day. The price to get in should have been a shilling (one five-pence piece in today's money) and sixpence for children (which is now two and a half new pence) then you got the tickets for the rides as you went in at the box office – as many as you could afford.

There were two ways in to the park: one from Hipperholme where they came by bus or by train and the other from Hove Edge by bus from Brighouse and by coach from as far away as Huddersfield, Bradford, Leeds and all the big towns and cities in the summer. The little Half House Lane was full of them, there would be thirty to forty a time going down into the park. If you walked in, it was about one mile from Hove Edge and the same from Hipperholme.

When you got in the park you walked through the lovely gardens and trees and down to the amusements. The gardens and trees were on the hillside. The flat part was where the two lakes were and the amusements were around them and grass to picnic. Around the amusements were aerial swings, a mountain slide, a little railway that went round the lakes and boats on both lakes and there were Swing Boats, Go-Karts and funny mirrors, also slot machines and a maze garden. There was an open-air theatre where they had variety shows and you had to sit on stone seats like in a Roman theatre. They had two shows a day and at the end of summer a firework display. It was sold after the war and was never the same afterwards.

Mrs Joan Thompson – Barnoldswick (recorded memory 8 August 1990)

two

'Are we there yet Dad?'

When Sunny Vale first opened to the public the only means of getting there for the majority of people was by horse and cart or to walk, both there and back. To walk several miles and often more from the outer communities of Halifax was commonplace. This 1902 procession through Hipperholme was part of the Coronation celebration for King Edward Vll and Queen Alexandra with all the local Sunday schools and organisations taking part. Then, as part of the celebrations, the marchers went on to join in the continued celebrations at Sunny Vale. This occasion was a good reason for everyone to go out in their Sunday best. Most of these children went on to visit Sunny Vale and become hooked on what was to be a place they would enjoy and visit time after time. As they got older they would then take their own children and in later years their grandchildren as well.

On Friday 7 November 1902 the Halifax Tramway was extended from Stump Cross to Hipperholme. This new form of transport was able to bring even greater numbers to enjoy the delights of Sunny Vale. Here one of the new tramcars approaches Hipperholme en route to Hove Edge and then on to Brighouse town centre

ENTERPRIZE TENT
I.O.R. Society, HANGING HEATON.

ANNUAL

EXCURSION

ON

Saturday, June 20th, 1931,

TO

SUNNY VALE
HIPPERHOLME.

In addition to all the popular Attractions and Amusements of the Pleasure Park,

Special Engagement of

FLOCKTON PRIZE BAND
To Play Selections and for Dancing.

A SPECIAL EXCURSION will be run as under :

BATLEY (L.M.S.)	**2-0**	**p.m.**
BATLEY CARR & STAINCLIFFE ...	**2-2**	,,
DEWSBURY (Wellington Road) ...	**2-6**	,,
RAVENSTHORPE & THORNHILL ...	**2-10**	,,

Returning from Hipperholme at 8-40 p.m.

Approximate Train Times only. Actual Times may be had from members of the Committee.

INCLUSIVE TICKETS for RAIL, ADMISSION and TEA only—ADULT MEMBERS AND FRIENDS, **2/3**

Juvenile Members FREE.

☞ *Accommodation in Tea Rooms Reserved for all Ticket Holders.*

Tickets may be had from any Member of the Committee, or Mr. J. W. SENIOR, *Secretary*, Woodland Cottage Hanging Heaton.

An Early Application for Tickets is desired.   ALL ARE WELCOME.

CONDITIONS OF ISSUE OF EXCURSION FARE TICKETS.

Excursion Tickets and Tickets issued at Fares less than the Ordinary Fares are issued subject to the Notices and Conditions shown in the Company's current Time Tables.

PLEASE RETAIN THIS BILL FOR REFERENCE.

Jackson & Clayton, Halifax.

The annual excursion to Sunny Vale was always something special and something the management promoted throughout the county. This 1931 handbill is an illustration of the kind of publicity they used on a regular basis. These handbills would have been handed out to children at Sunday schools to take home and show their parents. They would also have been available in tramcar waiting rooms as well as at railway stations. An interesting aspect of this handbill are the train times – for those readers who can remember this excursion route I have a feeling they would agree that in those days these times would have been well adhered to. Please note the letters IOR, which stand for Independent Order of Rechobites and was the Hanging Heaton Enterprise Tent (branch). The Flockton Prize Band was just one of many brass bands that provided the live music for the visitors to listen to and/or to dance to. The bands which provided entertainment were not just the small village bands; many of the bigger named brass bands also performed at Sunny Vale. As well as concert performances, bands also took part in brass band contests.

Opposite above: There were many sights and sounds on the road approaching Sunny Vale – Allen's Brickworks at the Hipperholme end of the valley was a thriving business for many years and when it was in full production visitors could not fail to be aware of this. For all the young ladies visiting and wearing their best dresses – no jeans in those days – you can imagine the problems they would have in keeping them clean with the continuous settlement of dust and dirt.

Hipperholme Railway Station opened on 1 August 1850 but was to see a huge increase in passengers once cheap excursions could be booked from most railway stations in Lancashire and Yorkshire to Hipperholme. An increasing number of special trains were being booked prior to each season opening. Large crowds poured off the 'specials' from Barnsley, Leeds, Keighley, Slaithwaite, Bradford, Lofthouse, Featherstone and much further afield as the reputation and success of Sunny Vale began to grow.

Memories of the Music

The very mention of Sunny Vale brings back wonderful memories for me – it was there that my parents first met. It would have been in the early 1920s when the pleasure gardens were a popular venue for young people to gather. My father was from Cleckheaton and my mother from Brighouse but her eldest sister and her husband farmed at Sunny Bank Farm, on the hilltop on the Halifax side of Sunny Vale, so mother was a frequent visitor to the area.

My main memories are of the music which could be heard a long way off. When we visited my aunt we could hear it as we descended from Hipperholme Station and all the way up the other side of the valley, to Sunny Bank farm.

Some time in the mid-thirties my aunt and uncle moved down to Lower Norcliffe farm which was adjacent to Sunny Vale itself. Between the farm and the boundary of the pleasure gardens was a tramway for trucks to transport from the nearby brickworks. I also seem to remember an overhead transport system for the same purpose.

Mrs Pat Oliver, née Carter – Gristhorpe, Filey Barnoldswick (recorded memory 3 August 2006). Please note that Mrs Oliver's cousin was the wife of the late Frank Nunn.

Life in the Valley

I lived and worked in the valley for many years and knew the owners of Bunces. I also knew most of the folks that worked there. I worked there myself with a horse and cart. One of the jobs was to take copper and silver to the bank at Hipperholme. My wife's parents Mr and Mrs Ben Bates delivered the milk there. I can remember the train trips that all came to Hipperholme Station.

They held brass band contests, there were hand-bell ringers, and one of the bands came from Shibden Hall Reformatory School, which closed down many years ago. It was in Lister Lane above the brickworks. I lived at Sunny Bank farm, later at Lower Norcliffe farm, the home of Mr and Mrs Ben Bates, and then I lived at No. 3 The Brownings, Sutcliffe Wood Road. Sunny Vale was a wonderful place – I saw it grow from something quite small to a very popular attraction.

Mr Frank Nunn (recorded memory 5 September 1990)

Opposite below: As the children poured out from the platform onto the top of the steep cobbled road their excitement grew even more intense when they heard the familiar strains of 'Little Sir Echo' being played out on the hurdy-gurdy machine by a one-legged man. Originally written in 1917 and recorded many times, this song was always a children's favourite. As each season began the hurdy-gurdy man took up his regular position leaning against the iron bridge above the station.

Whilst the children would not notice, being far too excited, parents – particularly those visiting for the first time – would be taking in all the sights and sounds as they walked down Station Road, the cobbled road down into the valley. One of those sights was this landmark mill complex. These were the premises of Joseph Wood & Sons Ltd, whose registered office was in Badger Lane, Hipperholme and was a worsted spinning company. Many of the workers at this mill, which no longer exists, would have taken their own children to the magical place known by them as Sunny Bunces. This would have certainly included my grandma, who worked there as a 'half-time' worker. This meant she would work in the mill half of the day and then attend school the second half – which half came first would vary.

The only road into the valley once the cobbled road ran out was to then turn left from Station Road into what is called Sutcliffe Wood Bottom Lane. The first houses on the left of this very early photograph are called Sunny Mount and are still there today. The block of houses on the right are called The

Brownings (built in around 1913) followed by 'Lake View', 'Lake Lea' and 'Brook Lynn', the former homes of Joseph Bunce and his two sons. Once having passed all these houses, visitors to Sunny Vale would begin to notice the number of people walking along with them would be gradually increasing and much noisier.

Looking across the bow of a steam-driven crane at one of Brooke's Halifax Road, Hove Edge quarries. The sight of the tramcar in the distance indicates that the photograph was taken after 16 April 1903, when the extended route out of Halifax from Stump Cross through to Brighouse reached Hove Edge. The only means of transport prior to the arrival of the tramcar was either by horse and cart or by walking. As many older readers will recall from their own childhoods, walking from one place to another, sometimes as many as several miles each way, was commonplace.

Once the new tramcar route had reached Hove Edge, extension of the route carried on and by February 1904 the new route from Halifax to Brighouse was completed, making travelling far easier and quicker. This new mode of transport helped the number of visitors to Sunny Vale to grow even more dramatically. This tramcar is in the centre of Hove Edge on what was obviously a quiet day, possibly out of season. On almost any other day this area would have been a sea of faces filling both sides of the road with countless children all trying to cross the road at once. From this point, to get down into the

Walterclough Valley you would turn left into Half House Lane, just behind the tramcar. Excited children could not get down into the valley fast enough. Mothers and grandmothers would walk down in a more sedate style, whilst the menfolk might just call at either the Dusty Miller or Joiners Arms public houses for a swift 'gill' (a gill was traditionally a half pint in Yorkshire pubs, although technically it was a quarter of a pint) of beer and then follow on.

Above, left and right: A familiar name to children who visited Sunny Vale would have been that of Ganson's Mineral Water Company (top left). This company was owned by Droylsden (Manchester), born William Gottleib Ganson (top right), and his wife Cheshire, born Caterina. He purchased the company in 1885 and was situated in a building next to the Joiners Arms (now the Hove Edge post office). It was from that warehouse that countless bottles of mineral water were carted down into the valley to quench the thirst of generations of children. William Ganson was a member of the inaugural Brighouse Borough Council in 1893. He died in 1904, and the company was then managed by his son Abraham. In 1927 the company was owned by Ernest Sheffield – during the 1930s local Hove Edge children always referred to the enclosed area round the back of the Ganson's as 'Pop Yard'. Abraham Ganson died in 1940 but by that time the business had moved into new premises on Half House Lane. In 1949 Ernest Sheffield sold the business. He died in 1957. In later years the Half House Lane site was used by Broadoak Garage and the Corona Soft Drinks Co.. The building is now used by Flow Technology Ltd.

Whilst researching this book I found that a number of people who visited as children could remember that halfway down the road into the valley bottom there was a very high wall. This wall was originally built in 1889 to prevent landslip and the road being blocked. However, something else many people also remember was a perpendicular stone column on the opposite side of the road to the high wall. Some people have told me they could remember trucks flying across the valley down to a mine. 'Have I dreamt that?' many have asked. Certainly not – and these two photographs prove it. The trucks or tubs, as seen above, were at what its owners, Brooke's Stone Co., called the 'Flight' and were on a pulley system which carried the empty trucks across the road and, with the assistance of the perpendicular column, carried the trucks suspended on cables down in the bottom to the Walterclough Pit.

The photograph on the right shows the trucks being carried down into the valley. The clean stonework is the perpendicular column which everyone visiting Sunny Vale from Hove Edge remembers. For many young boys it was exciting to see one of the trucks come off the cables and crash down into the valley below. However, in the course of my research I have met one person who can recall as a small child riding inside one of the trucks down into the valley bottom – just thinking about the risks involved is enough to give you a frightening shiver.

What a Thrill

In 1953, the year of the Coronation, I was seven years old and on a number of occasions I had watched some of the mine workers ride down to the pit sat inside the tubs – I thought 'what a great idea'. One day I decided to have a go myself and I did, it was both frightening and very exciting. I only did it the once but what a thrill. Little did I know then that many years later I would once again be visiting the valley during the days of the stock racing, when I was involved in the organisation.
Brian Fox – Brighouse (recorded memory October 2006)

Opposite below: This road would have been awash with children who would be running down the hill or walking in a more orderly hand in hand, two by two, snake fashion under the control of their Sunday school teachers. For all those children who had been before, at this point the excitement would have been clearly visible on their beaming faces. Once they passed this large property, 'Essendyne House', it was the point of no return. Sunny Bunces, here we come…

In the bottom of the valley the trucks which had not come off the cables and crashed arrived at Walterclough Pit. This pre-1920 photograph of the pit head shows some of the miners from that period. Originally opened in 1888, Brooke's Stone Company bought the pit in 1906 and it closed in February 1969.

The sight of these two lakes means that we have finally arrived at our destination. For many children visiting in the early years, the lower lake, the Victoria Lake and the upper Alexandra Lake would have been the greatest expanse of water they had ever seen. The smoking chimneys are at Allan's Brickworks – after being open for almost a century it finally closed down in 1988.

Seasonal Sports

My memories of Sunny Vale date back to the 1930s when I was living with my family in Halifax. What I remember the most was the two lakes. There was boating in the summer and ice-skating in the winter. We never developed the great skill needed to ice-skate quick enough because it had usually melted away.
Hilary Pedley – Oldfield, Keighley (recorded memory 2 September 1990)

three

Victoria & Alexandra

Having arrived you would now have had to join what would have seemed to be an endless queue to get in through one of the turnstiles. There were a number of ways to get into Sunny Vale but only the one, tried and tested way where small children could get in without paying...

This photograph was taken in around 1903 and shows how nicely the gardens and walkways had been laid out by Joseph Bunce and his team of gardeners; a skill he had been taught by his father.

Sunny Vale without paying

Living in Southowram meant access into Sunny Vale without paying was easy. We did have a little money, but free entry meant an extra ride on the boat swings or slide, so Mr Bunce got our money one way or another.

Mrs Marlene Ward, née Shackleton (recorded memory 11 August 2006)

Above: As you walked through the avenue of rhododendron and holly bushes following what were once the contours of the network of footpaths, it was a very scenic journey. Throughout the time of peak season, visitors would have found it difficult just to pass each other. Today, though the footpaths have long since disappeared, looking closely at the dense overgrowth where nature has taken its course, there is still some evidence that something else was here.

Below: Continuing our journey into the valley bottom we are now passing these buildings – it was in this building where those visitors who had pre-booked their teas would form an orderly queue for their plate of quartered sandwiches, cup of tea and a bun or piece of cake.

A mountain of salmon sandwiches

One lovely day in 1935 my grandparents took me to Sunny Vale. It was warm, the wasps were about as we sat having soft drinks whilst sat outside at a wooden table – they were very off-putting. Later we all went into the café where granddad ordered salmon salads for us. Alas, when the waitress arrived she brought a veritable mountain of salmon sandwiches instead – what a blow it was – but we ate them all.
Mrs Joyce Foster - Blackpool (recorded memory September 1990)

At last we are almost there; we are now in the lower drive, surrounded on both sides by holly and rhododendron bushes. This is the same footpath you all went home by and as you reached the bend at the top, one last look over your shoulder and you would have been entranced by all the fairy lights which encircled the large lake at the end of the season. It was also the same footpath by which young ladies would make their way home, with no fear or sense of trepidation – you were in a different time then, with little to no worries about personal safety.

Now you had a multi-choice decision to make – did you go to the smaller Victoria Lake or the larger Alexandra Lake or follow the sign to the Maze? For a small child it was almost too much to take in; it is no wonder that so many visitors called it a magical playground.

A Saturday September surprise

I lived in Elland as a child with my four brothers and my mum, until my dad came home from the war in 1945. What a Saturday September surprise. Dad told us all to brush and polish our shoes after breakfast – no mention of why. I remember we all went to the bus stop; we waited patiently, what a welcome sight when the bus finally arrived. When we got off the bus we had to walk a fair distance to the turnstile. We had no idea where we were but dad said with a smile on his face, 'we're at Sunny Vale'. We couldn't stop talking and laughing. What a wonderful place – my favourite ride was taking my heavy mat, sitting on it and coming down the slide – and no burnt bum either. I remember rowing a boat, with my brothers and dad watching on. My brothers thought they saw a peacock – we argued about it. 'No, it's a swan', I said. We rowed over to an island where the swan was, my brother Jack fell in the water as we got nearer to the island. Later we went in the Maze and I got lost – a kind man guided me out and back to my mum and dad. We went on the boat swings – trying to reach the sky. Eventually dad said it was time to go home, it was such a surprise, our first holiday – Sunny Bunces will always be so special to me.
Mrs Margaret Barker, née Walmsley – Greetland (recorded memory August 2006)

Sunny Vale's first season saw some two to three hundred visitors, mainly from Halifax and Brighouse. At the close of the first season a small lake (the Victoria Lake) was constructed, it was just one third the size of the above lake. In 1883 it was extended but owing to the increasing popularity of the gardens and the additional number of boats placed upon the lake it become too congested.

Many people remember the Victoria Lake being frozen over every winter – this saw many of them venture out onto the ice wearing ice-skates. Accompanied by the echoing sounds of Emile Waldteufel's composition, *Les Patineurs Valse* Op. 183 — better known to these visitors as 'The Skaters' Waltz'. The music, laughter and no doubt a few moans and groans would be heard throughout the valley. This photograph was taken during the early 1930s. The lady in the foreground is Mrs Lucy Heaton, who lived in St Giles Road, Hove Edge and later in Bracken Road, Brighouse and visited Sunny Vale regularly throughout the summer and winter, just as her family was to do in later years.

The first boat used on the Victoria Lake came from Huntingdon and, being too long to turn, was rowed backward and forward along the lake. In 1892 twenty acres were added to the estate and the Southowram side of the stream utilised as a dance ground. Five years later the large upper Alexandra Lake was opened, the construction of which had necessitated the purchase of two additional acres of land. The lake was four acres in extent, 256 metres long by 55 to 73 metres wide, and the promenade around the lake had the capacity to accommodate 8,000 visitors. The construction of the lake, including the alteration of the beck course, took over two years to complete.

As the children look on, the brass band plays, sometime between 1900 and 1910. It is not possible to say which brass band it is even after enhancing the edge of the big bass drum. Brass bands were the live music at Sunny Vale, with different bands being engaged to play every weekend. The management not only held concerts and provided the dance music but they also organised band contests. The last band contest was held in 1938 – the senior class winners were the Hebden Bridge Band and the junior class winners were the now defunct Cragg Vale Band.

Whilst it was the rowing boats that were the most popular on the lower Victoria Lake, it was on this lake that young children had the opportunity of being taken on a bigger boat – the launch, or a ship as many of them called it.

Fishing for sticklebacks

During the early 1940s I used to walk down to Sunny Vale from our house in Slead Syke, Brighouse, with my parents, brothers and sisters. We would always take time to play around the boating lakes, catching sticklebacks; then we would always throw them back in.

Mr Keith Mountain – Sheffield (recorded memory August 1990)

No, this is not a remake of Humphrey Bogart's *The African Queen* – it is the launch (or steamer, as it was officially called) which gave pleasure rides on the large Alexandra Lake. Having the opportunity of being taken for a ride on it was a real treat. Most children who visited Sunny Vale, particularly in the early years, would never have experienced this kind of boat ride before.

During the 1960s I remember meeting people who had gone on package holidays to Spain. Listening to them when they returned I heard about a boat that was operated and powered by foot pedals – these were called pedalos and they were new. This photograph of the Victoria Lake shows Sunny Vale's 1920s version of the pedalo and as many former visitors have told me, these were not operated by foot pedals but by hand-operated pedals.

Pedal power on the Victoria Lake, c. 1938. The young girl on the left is Miss Muriel Whitley, but who is the girl she is with? Sadly her name has long been forgotten.

What laughter there was

I lived in Ovenden, Halifax from 1929 until the 1950s and went to Sunny Vale just the once. I remember my aunt taking me with another child, whose name I cannot remember now. I well remember however the pedal boat. What laughter there was until we finally managed to get our pedals co-ordinated.
Mrs Muriel Wood, née Whitley – Crossflatts, Bingley (recorded memory August 2006)

All aboard! Over a dozen visitors enjoy a 1930s trip out on the launch. Looking at the fashions of the day, you were obviously not in fashion unless you were wearing a hat. The Sunny Vale Helter-Skelter dominates this scene – in 1955 when the Sunny Vale site contents were sold at public auction, it is recorded in *The Brighouse Echo* newspaper that this particular item was sold to an unknown buyer for £8.15: just what happened to it after it was sold, no one seems to know.

Wartime security

During the war years when the winters were sometimes more severe with heavy snow and strong frost, weather forecasts were forbidden because of wartime security procedures. If there was a period of full moon an advertisement would appear in the *Halifax Evening Courier*, which read 'Shibden Park 7 p.m. and Sunny Vale 7 p.m.'. This meant to the locals that there was skating on the frozen lakes at both locations.

Richard Hallawell (recorded memory September 2006)

As the years went by the popularity of Sunny Vale began to expand beyond all expectations, particularly from 1904 with the advent of tramcar travel. In those days most of the visitors were from Sunday schools and other organisations from throughout the county. As the dark clouds of war were gathering over Europe you could be forgiven for thinking that with so many young men going to war that from 1914 the popularity of Sunny Vale would have begun to drop off. Throughout the war years it is said that the Bunce family distributed free tickets to those families who had loved ones involved in the war. It was this gesture that helped to maintain spirits, particularly amongst younger children and, of course, to keep Sunny Vale going.

Times were changing – the war years made sure of that, and people's expectations were beginning to be greater. The possibility of visiting the east and west seaside coastal resorts was soon to become a reality.

A present from Sunny Vale

I am now seventy-three years of age and visited Sunny Vale in 1924–1925 when I attended Sunday school in a little village called Dungworth, which is about seven miles from Sheffield, from where we used have a trip each year. For many years I cherished a ball which I won and was inscribed with the words 'a present from Sunny Vale'. I remember being there with my grandma and being lost in the Maze and being afraid that I might miss the charabanc home.
Mrs Hilda Shepherd – Bradfield Dale, Sheffield (recorded memory 27 August 1990)

Opposite below: What do you do with a boat once it is beyond its intended use? Firewood, perhaps? No, they did not waste anything at Sunny Vale. Look at the boat on the edge of the lake, whilst these children take part in a race. Perhaps there are anxious relatives watching on in an upturned boat which has been recycled to be a seat with a degree of shelter from the elements.

The end of the First World War could have seen the demise of Sunny Vale. With potentially less and less people visiting, there might have been a gradual decline and then closure. With so many of their male pre-war visitors not returning home or being mentally or physically shattered from their wartime experiences, many of the organisations these young men had once belonged to never recovered and didn't restart after the war. It was, however, the Sunday schools who continued to use Sunny Vale as their Annual Summer Treat for the children. Needless to say, with the onset of the 1920s something else was going to impact on Sunny Vale's popularity – the pull of the real seaside was getting stronger year by year. In 1928, 2,000 employees and their families were taken on an expenses-paid trip to Blackpool by Blakeborough Valves of Brighouse. On their return they had the taste for more; the days of boarding houses, paying extra for the cruet set and taking your own food and bedding had arrived.

The one thing that Sunny Vale could not afford to do was to be complacent. 'If it's not broke why mend it?' This is a phrase we have all heard before. But if nothing changes or improves customers will go elsewhere; this was something that the Bunce family were well aware of. Water cycling was hardly a 'white-knuckle ride' but it was an added attraction. I am sure if such a ride was available today swimsuits would have been almost compulsory and not your best three-piece suit, Albert watch and chain, the shiniest boots in the district and a new flat cap from the Co-op. It is interesting to see that it was not a ride for the young ladies.

From the early days when the brass bands used to play and entertain the visitors from a platform in front of the lake, here we see they have now got a traditional bandstand. Having played in brass bands for almost fifty years I often smile when playing in a bandstand. They always have a nice tiled roof but from years of experience I can state that the wind and rain never come down vertically but always blow from the left or right. Any bandsperson will tell you that it is compulsory to have six of your mother's clothes pegs to hold down the music to the music stand and a firm boot to stand on the music stand to prevent it from blowing away: a practice brass band players will still (when they remember) adhere to nowadays.

These spectators are the lucky ones; speed-boat racing was not a regular visitor attraction at Sunny Vale but on this occasion the Alexandra Lake was being used for testing purposes.

What a sight for the visitors as Douglas Miller (in the white shirt), a member of the well-known Brighouse family and someone who was a very keen boat enthusiast, is sitting on the bank looking on anxiously as the engine from one of his speed boats is being recovered from the Alexandra Lake onto the rowing boat.

Just what this large crowd gathered around the top lake are looking at remains a mystery; although there is a young person in the water, I don't believe they are gathered for that event – from the style of clothes everyone is wearing, the date would be the pre-1920s. At the end of each season the Bunce family would close the year with a re-enactment of some event on the large lake. This could take the form of something local, national or even an international event.

Sinking ship and angels' song

In 1912 we lived in Southowram. One day my mother and dad took my sister and myself along with another family down Barker Royd fields which overlooked Bunces, from where we had a full view of all that was happening. I remember the *Titanic* sinking – a bit jerky but still very emotional. Standing on the island around the sinking ship were children dressed as angels singing 'Nearer my God to Thee'. An event I have never forgotten.

Mrs E. Farrow — Grimsby (recorded memory from 1990)

Looking at this photograph of the same scene, there are a number of new attractions, many of which made their first appearance during the early 1930s. Then of course there were the Silver Jubilee celebrations of King George V and Queen Mary, when once again free tickets were handed to many of the local children. Throughout this period the dark clouds over Europe were gathering again when once more the nation's young men would go to war. Would Sunny Vale survive just as it did after the First World War?

Having already seen one example of an event taking place on the top lake, just imagine you are once again eight years old and you have spent the afternoon at Sunny Bunces. On arriving back home you say to your mother, 'mum, we have seen a giant swan at Sunny Vale, it was as big as our house'. Well I am sure you can imagine the response of disbelief you would get from your mother – but to a small child that was the magic of Sunny Vale.

Standing with her swimming cap in her hand to the left-hand side of the man in the middle is Greta Imeson (née Smith) and standing to her left is her teammate of those days, Jean Megson. Their swimming coach was Esther Sandford who is standing at the back of the group of onlookers. The other youngsters in the photograph came from various swimming clubs in the Yorkshire No. 3 District, as it was then known. This occasion was the No. 3 District Open Water Long Distance Swimming Trials. This was a first-time effort for Greta and her friends who were members of the Lockwood Ladies from the Ramsden Street Baths in Huddersfield. The following year the event was transferred from Sunny Vale top lake to Sparth Reservoir at Marsden, on the outskirts of Huddersfield.

Mrs Ada Webster posing alongside the top lake – with the Glacier ride in the background set against the valley side. Judging from the coats the youngsters are wearing behind her and no leaves on the trees it was not taken in midsummer.

Through Fairy Glen to Bunces

I can remember 'Sunny Bunces' from a very early age being taken there during the school holidays as a 'treat' by my parents – I am now eighty-two years old. We took the Halifax bus from Thornton Square in Brighouse and we got off at Hove Edge and walked down what we called 'Fairy Glen' to Bunces.

I recall in 1935 – the King George V Jubilee, all school children were given a 'free day'. There were free vouchers for the rides: Helter-Skelter, Aerial Glider and rowing boats just to name a few. There was a roller-skating rink. I visited often when I was between thirteen and fifteen years old. I can also recall Roy Castle singing 'The Sun Has Got His Hat On'; he was performing with a dancing school.

Mrs A. Webster née Brook – York (recorded memory December 2006)

SUNNY VALE GARDENS, HIPPERHOLME.

Sunny Vale.

SUNNY VALE GARDENS, HIPPERHOLME.

SUNNY VALE GARDENS, HIPPERHOLME.

Postcards were first introduced in Austria, from around 1869. The idea of the postcard was to allow people to communicate with each other, the emphasis being briefly and cheaply. Being a single sheet of fairly lightweight card, they were cheaper to send through the postal system than a standard letter. This was no doubt one of the key factors in ensuring they would be popular amongst the general population in Victorian and Edwardian Britain. Within a year the postcard was introduced into Great Britain – no pictures, no decorated cards: the first postcards were just plain pieces of card with the address on one side and the message on the other and could only be issued by the post office and bearing a pre-printed stamp. A major turning point came in 1894 when the Post Office gave up their monopoly on the publishing of all postcards and began to allow postcards to be published privately. They could, however, only be sent through the postal system with a self-adhesive stamp as proof that the postage had been paid. With these changes the thirst for sending postcards by the British public instead of sending letters saw the number of postcards passing through the postal system rocket to huge numbers. It also saw the introduction of illustrated postcards – however this was limited due to the lack of space owing to the insistence by the Post Office that one side of the card could only be for the address. In 1902 for the first time the Post Office allowed the back of postcards to be split down the centre allowing a person to write the address on the right-hand side and a brief message on the left-hand side. This then allowed the front of the postcard to have an even larger image of either a picture or some decorative artwork – ensuring the postcard was to become even more popular. The owners of Sunny Vale had a number of postcards produced in the early days but as this example shows they were rather amateur-looking. In the 1950s, the Ripponden company Lilywhite Ltd produced postcards of Sunny Vale along with almost every other town, village and community in the United Kingdom. These were produced to a far more professional finish. During the 1960s Lilywhite's became part of A.H. Leach, photographic finishers in Brighouse. Today the old Lilywhite postcards are much sought-after and can command relatively high prices at postcard fairs and amongst postcard collectors. Collectors will be saddened to hear that all the original photographic glass plates of those old postcards no longer exist.

Above left: A receipt from Charles Kershaw's Slead Syke Nurseries for £14.4s.7d dated 2 October 1929.

Above right: A 3d Sunny Vale token.

Sunny Vale had many items both for sale and that could be won on sideshows. This early postcard enabled visitors to send a message back home to tell their friends what a lovely time they were having. With twice-a-day postal collections and deliveries, many visitors to Sunny Vale would send a postcard back home or buy them as a collectable. With the huge numbers still visiting Sunny Vale the level of publicity these postcards generated throughout the North of England would give the name of Sunny Vale Pleasure Gardens an unprecedented level of advertising exposure.

My friend made her guess and won

I have happy memories of Sunny Vale – I was born and lived in Krumlin, Barkisland, near Halifax. I remember the Krumlin Brass Band used to play there twice every year; I used to watch the band playing in the bandstand. We used to get there by charabanc and had to get out at the top of the main road as it was too dangerous a hill to ride down. I loved to row over the lakes; I would be eleven or twelve years old when I first started to go down there and I am now eighty-one. There were some lovely concerts, all in the open air – I remember the roller-skating, Helter-Skelter and the Puzzle Gardens. There were the slot machines near to where you could buy cakes, sandwiches and drinks. I also remember going there after I was married and then lived at Sowood which is near Stainland. On one visit we took part in a competition to guess how many people were there, which was run by the *Halifax Courier*. After I made my guess, me and my friends went round counting small groups of people. My friend made her guess and won the fifteen shillings which was well appreciated considering her husband was out of work; it was a lot of money in 1934. In later years I took my son and travelled from Greetland Station to Hipperholme Station – such happy days.

Mrs H. Dyson – Hambleton, Blackpool (recorded memory 1 September 1990)

four

All the Fun
of the Fair

As each group of children arrived, one of the grown-ups from their Sunday school party would give them each a number of tickets. These would entitle them to a number of free rides. Well, the children thought they were free, but in reality they had all been pre-paid.

My father seemed to know everyone

My earliest recollections of Sunny Bunces, as it was known, must date to around 1938 – just before the war. Living in Halifax, to be told we were going to Sunny Vale caused great excitement. Picnics had to be prepared, then the walk down to the Halifax railway station in the valley bottom to catch a train to Hipperholme. What a long journey it seemed to me – stopping at North Bridge Station, going through the Beacon tunnel, out past Shibden Park to arrive at Hipperholme Station. The pleasure grounds were just a short walk down the cobbled lane.

My father seemed to know everyone – he printed the tickets and all the advertising posters, so we often had these to deliver. He also liked to lend a hand in his spare time running a stall. So we were allowed in through the tall turnstile free of charge. Whether we got in free or we had to pay, these were some of the best times of my childhood years.

The first amusement was immediately inside the entrance. This was a horseshoe-shaped monorail from which hung chairs on long poles. Once you were seated in one of these, it then set off, gathering speed down its gentle slope. This may sound tame by today's standards but as it travelled down it came to dipped sections in the rail, which made the chair move erratically before regaining its course.

Mrs Barbara Lister née Holden – Brighouse (recorded memory 5 September 1990)

Saturday afternoons at Sunny Vale

This photograph of mum (Mrs Mary Wells) and me sitting in the Swing Boat ride takes me back to those days as a child when mum used to close our family shop in Brighouse on Saturday afternoons and then take us down to Sunny Vale. I had an extra special time if mum would let my best friend Marvene come with us and we could have a picnic. The Helter-Skelter ride was my favourite. Then on the way home as we walked up the hill so we could call at Ripley's Ice Cream factory for a lolly.

Marlene Travis, née Wells – Brighouse (recorded memory December 2006)

As the number of visitors continued to grow, improved and more sophisticated attractions were added. Throughout the 1920s groups of people continued to visit but peoples' lives were changing. Even though the twenties were tough times, people's expectations were beginning to be higher. Considering what life had been like forty years earlier this new generation were now a little bit better off. Here we see a group of adults posing for the photographer. Please note the small child behind them who is about to step into the roundabout car, hopefully before it sets off.

The corner of the amusements – remember those slot machines where you would insert your penny, watch for the ball bearing to drop down and give the lever a flick and the machine wins again? How many readers can remember keeping one eye on the ground, where you might find the odd penny some lucky winner had lost – no such luck, just one thing left to try, 'mum, can I have some money?'

Who were the motorcycle heroes of the 1950s – John Surtees and Mike Hailwood? This is three-year old David Brown of Henry Street, Brighouse in 1953, and he fancies being the next world champion. It is probably as well he is not looking over his shoulder at the girl rider, who might be his sister Julie, showing off a bit, 'look no hands'. Not even his older brother Phillip on the motorcycle even further behind is watching her either.

Throughout the 1930s Sunny Vale saw continued success – the most memorable event for the thousands of visitors was that of the Silver Jubilee celebrations of 1935.

A lemonade bottle exploded in my hand

Yes indeed I remember 'Sunny Bunces' very well, especially about 1935. About a week before King George V's Jubilee whilst playing in a wigwam with friends, a glass lemonade bottle exploded in my hand, resulting in chloroform stitches sat on the settee. This didn't deter me from going to 'Sunny Bunces' about a week later to spend my free tickets we had all been given at Lightcliffe National School. As I remember we all got twelve free rides and a commemorative beaker with portraits of King George and Queen Mary on to take home.

Mr Derek Cordingley – Cullingworth (recorded memory 12 August 2006)

The Glacier – the nearest Sunny Vale came to having a white-knuckle ride. You had to 'get a mat', as the sign boldly points out. You must remember this was not your modern synthetic type of mat either but your original prickly coconut mat. No doubt having been there all season it would be full of grit and soaking wet on those unforgettable rainy days. You went up one side on a cable pulley clinging onto your mat, as all the water from it ran down your legs. Once at the top and taking your mat to the downward slope you would then sit on it hoping for the ride of your life. Alas, with the rain and damp weather, no such luck, only a slow jerky ride to the bottom. However, on the days the sun was truly 'cracking the flags' you would sit on your mat and fly down the chute. For those a little scared who might now be wondering how to slow down – friction burns prevented you from gripping the rails. Never fear, help was at hand – the chink in the run halfway down acted like a gravity brake, which ensured in those days before it became universally fashionable

that ladies wore jeans and trousers, they almost came to a dead stop. This meant momentarily losing control of their limbs, with arms and legs spread, the casual observer might be forced to ask the question, 'what are those boys all standing at the bottom of the chute for?' I will leave that to your imagination! No mention of health and safety in those days and certainly no mention at all of where the 'spells' might have ended up.

Eileen and Mary Jackson have happy memories of what in 1943 would have been their first experience on 'The Glacier', a so-called 'white-knuckle ride' (on the above photograph Eileen is on the right with Mary on the left). Travelling to Sunny Vale in those days meant two bus rides from their home in Shipley.

There wasn't one mirror that made me look nice

After getting off the bus at Hipperholme it seemed such a long walk down the steep cobbled hill and we could see such long queues at the turnstiles as we finally got nearer. We liked going on this bumpy slide, it was a bit scary – but good fun. There was a Hall of Mirrors and the first time Eileen went in, then aged six, she looked very seriously at the distortions in the mirrors. When she got out her mother asked what she thought about it, Eileen replied, 'why wasn't there one that made me look nice' – a comment that Eileen has never managed to live down.

Mrs Eileen Howe, née Jackson — Beverley, Nr Hull (recorded memory 1 August 2006)

This building is the roller-skating rink and was opened for the 1909 season along with the new dance floor. It is likely that the skating rink was created as a direct result of James Farnell Bunce's involvement with the old Empire Theatre in Atlas Mill Road, Brighouse, which he owned for a short time and was one of the first roller-skating rinks in Brighouse.

A rare view of the roller-skating rink interior – the new rink was designed by local architects Edwin Taylor & Son, who had offices in both Brighouse and Halifax. An unconfirmed story was that the skating rink surface in the very early days was covered in black lead. For those readers who are not familiar with black lead, this was traditionally something that 'mother' would have used to bring that extra sparkle to the old Yorkshire Range which was a combination of an oven, fireplace and water boiler.

One of the most popular features at Sunny Vale was the outdoor dancing that was particularly enjoyed by the ladies. Note all the young men standing at the back, no doubt lacking the courage and hoping that some young lady would ask them to dance. This

was in the days before piped music and the live music of the day was provided by one of the many brass bands that would be engaged to perform and provide entertaining music both for dancing and as general background music. Looking at this photograph we can see how things have changed – how many ladies can boast they have actually danced in the open air with a man in a bowler hat?

On closer examination the signboard to the right of the bandstand says 'Two Step' but no one is dancing. The local newspapers would visit Sunny Vale on a weekly basis to capture a few memorable images for the following week's edition. Here the dancing has stopped whilst the photographer captures the moment. Note the fashion of the day – everyone is wearing a hat.

Take your partners – another dance, a different era but still, a hat is just a real fashion accessory. Throughout the history of Sunny Vale there were many group bookings from organisations from across the North of England. Here are three memories from members of just three of the visiting organisations:

A trip into the countryside

We were collected from outside the Talmud Torah Hebrew School (a junior school for Jewish children in which they are taught Hebrew, Bible study and the other elements of Judaism) in Leeds one Sunday morning and taken by coach to Sunny Vale. This in itself was an adventure, as a trip into the countryside for us ten-year olds was a real treat. On our arrival we were given some fruit to eat during the day. We were also given some tickets which had to be given to whoever was operating the rides we wanted to go on. At the end of the day we were taken home and greeted by our parents – from the reception they gave us you would have thought that we had been to Australia and back. That is now sixty-eight years ago but that day is still a very vivid memory for me.
Mr Stan Miller – Leeds (recorded memory October 2005)

Pudsey Owls visit Sunny Vale

I remember visiting Sunny Vale just the once in 1947 – I was a member of Pudsey Owls Cycling Club. The two things I remember in particular were a local dancing class who were performing on the open-air stage and then a concert party who performed 'Pedro the Fisherman' amongst other items. I also spent some time on the roller-skating rink – it was such fun. Whilst many of us did enjoy our visit, the more serious members of our club were complaining about spending their time there and not doing some hard cycling.
Molly Lythe – Idle, Bradford (recorded memory August 1990)

A real treat to watch

The very mention of Sunny Vale takes me back to my childhood days in the 1920s and '30s when mum and dad would take me there for the day. My husband used to go there too. He went with a group from the Salvation Army in Bradford. Boarding a train at Bowling junction and then leaving the train at Hipperholme Station, what excitement, football in the field, cricket and rounders, the couples on the roller-skating rink or on the open-air dance floor it was a real treat to watch.
Mrs A. Hill – Clayton, Bradford (recorded memory August 1990)

As the youngsters danced the afternoon away, parents and grandparents would watch on, listening to the live music of the brass band. The large building in the background was the amusement arcade area where you could spend a few pennies on the slot machines. Those were the machines where you would place your penny in the slot and then watch the steel ball drop through a hole. Whether you gave the spring-loaded lever a full flick, half flick or you were one of those people who thought they knew just how much pressure to use on the lever to ensure the steel ball travelled round the machine and then landed in one of the end slots which would then pay you out the princely sum of six pence. Having watched these so-called slot machine experts many times, more often than not, however much they tried, they could not prevent the steel ball from finding its way down one of the centre slots which, as many of you will remember, paid out no winnings at all. The open-air dance stage was constructed in 1904 from the timber which had been originally used in the construction of the old Theatre Royal, Halifax. The stage was large enough to comfortably allow thirty couples to dance, without knocking each other over. This was one of Sunny Vale's popular attractions, particularly on Saturdays and holidays. Another feature of the rapidly changing Sunny Vale, especially from those pre-First World War years, was the illuminated carnivals, which were before the days of the soon-to-be-more-famous modern-day staged displays at Blackpool in 1912. In 1906 the structural work of the Palace of Illusions at the Bradford Exhibition was purchased and erected in the grounds. Comments recorded in the local newspaper and attributed to members of the Bunce family said that before the close of the 1906 season or before the opening of the following season they hoped to adopt some system of illuminating the pavilions and grounds. This was in response to the ever-increasing numbers attending Sunny Vale before the First World War.

Painting all the railings surrounding Sunny Vale

I am now seventy-nine but I well remember being taken to Sunny Vale as a very little girl by my parents and with my sister Jessie. My main recollection is the boating lakes, I think we probably went there at Easter time as I do know we were always with crowds of people; there were many in queues to hire the boats and go on the rides. My father, Horace Graydon, had a shop at No. 3 Hanson Lane in Halifax where he sold paint, and wallpaper. He was a master painter, decorator and undertaker. I remember one year he submitted a tender for the job of painting all the railings surrounding Sunny Vale. I don't know whether he was successful in getting the job – I am sure it was before the First World War, a long time ago.
Miss Mabel Graydon – Fairlight, Nr Hastings (recorded memory October 1990)

Above: This Edwardian photograph was taken at Sunny Vale in 1903 and shows the ever-popular Swing Boat ride. These were the same Swing Boats that the visitors who went in the early post-Second World War years would have enjoyed using as well. As each season came to an end the Bunce family would carefully dismantle the Swing Boats and take them inside during the winter months and as the new season drew nearer they would be given a fresh coat of paint to ensure they always looked their best for the new season's visitors.

Left: The Aerial Glider – seen here in the 1920s, well before the days of health and safety regulations. The seat for this bumpy ride was suspended from overhead – here are three small children about to sample the delights of this ride with the attendant standing by to calm their nerves – note there is no safety lap rail in front of them. Whilst the children at either side could hold on to the upright rails the youngster in the middle had nothing to hold on to other than the other two passengers.

Although Sunny Vale was still busy during the war years, in 1946 the family decided to sell it, they hoped, to the Brighouse Borough Council. Newspaper reports quoted an asking price of £20,000 and it was suggested that people were queuing up to buy it. Following a number of advertisements in the *Show World* magazine, attractive offers were made by a number of private individuals who were interested. In early 1946 the council gave it some consideration but with some councillors wanting to buy it but many others against spending the money, the writing was on the wall and after much deliberation it was decided that they would not buy it. It was finally sold to Fred Thompson, a fairground caterer from Cleveleys. Whilst Peter Bunce (the son of James

Farnell Bunce) on returning from his Royal Navy war service hoped to take it over from the family, this was not to be. He was given the job of manager by Fred Thompson and was in charge of the day-to-day running of the place. Sadly, whilst under the tenure of Fred Thompson the once almost magical Sunny Vale Pleasure Gardens was destined never be the same again.

Strange machines called Gee-Bikes

I remember sitting watching the brass bands in the bandstand and listening to all the lively music they seemed to always play. The indoor roller-skating rink was always packed with excited youngsters. Next to this was an outdoor wooden rink which held all my favourite amusements and this was where my father usually helped out. It was here where the bicycles with a difference were – these special bicycles required no pedalling – the foot rests were static. To propel the machine you had to bounce up and down on the saddle all the time – these strange machines were called 'Gee-Bikes' because of the horse-riding action. Doing this and keeping your balance was quite a feat.

Mrs Barbara Lister, née Holden – Brighouse (recorded memory September 2006)

'The Flyer' – this ride must have been quite terrifying to all those young children who tried it out for the first time. Built on the hillside, the faster you went, the higher you went. The base of the steel construction was enclosed on all four sides and covered with a galvanised roof to create a small building; this was the home of the ponies and donkeys. Once the public auction of got under way in 1955 and everything went under the hammer, The Flyer was dismantled and sold for scrap. The only part that remains today is the building at the base, where until recent years you could still see sections of the original steel structure which managed to hold the original building upright.

Nature has returned and taken over this scene – it is difficult to imagine this corner of Sunny Vale was once a picture of activity of anxious parents watching on as their children would sample the delights of the nerve-tingling ride opposite

Whilst little evidence remains today that Sunny Vale Pleasure Gardens, the amusements or rides ever existed, if you look carefully through the dense undergrowth you can just about manage to find little bits of its past – even though the whole site has almost returned to its original natural state and is now almost completely overgrown. In these two photographs which were taken in recent years you can see just how much this part of the site has returned to nature. This is the same view you were looking at on page fifty-eight. The Flyer may have long since been scrapped but the home of the ponies and donkeys is still there.

Looking now at this photograph of a group of children, who were no doubt posing for the newspaper photographer, you can imagine what the mother of the little boy at the bottom of the Helter-Skelter ride must have said to him about him pulling a funny face when it appeared in the local newspaper.

Down the Helter-Skelter on coconut mats

Between 1937 (when I was eleven) and 1944 we lived at Park Place, off Parkinson Lane, Halifax. In the earlier part of this period I used to go to Sunny Vale with my friend Rita Cullen. As Rita's father worked on the railways at Halifax Station we were able to get free rail passes from Halifax to Hipperholme. I remember as we queued at one of the turnstiles we could see people sliding down the Helter-Skelter on coconut mats. They all looked to be really enjoying themselves, just as we did when we got our mats and went on it.
Miss Alison Brooks – Wark, Hexham (recorded memory 14 August 2006)

In this early post-Second World War photograph, Jimmy Wells and his eldest daughter Marlene have quite clearly had enough. But, as Marvene Thornton, Marlene's best friend looks into the camera, her thoughts would evidently have been on wanting Mr Wells to wake up and take them to explore more of the delights, on what was one of their early visits to Sunny Bunces

Sunday School Treats at Sunny Vale

As youngsters before the war days (1939), Doris, who was to be my future wife, went to the Ebenezer church at Bailiff Bridge, whilst I attended All Saints in Halifax. Both of our Sunday school 'Treats' were at Sunny Vale. From Bailiff Bridge they would walk but we walked to the Halifax Railway Station and caught the train to Hipperholme. Once we got into the grounds we were sold tickets – 1d each or 9d for a dozen. These tickets could be used to pay for the different rides and for boat rides.
Harold Hayton – Middlesbrough (recorded memory December 1990)

The traditional Gallopers Roundabout – which was to both excite and scare children, as it went round and round. Even though it may have been a bit scary, there is no doubt that the same children would have been hoping there was just one more ticket left...

This corner view of the Sunny Vale Amusement Park dates back to pre-1946. The traditional Gallopers Roundabout was installed by Fred Thompson who had bought the Sunny Vale complex earlier that year. The Aerial Glider ride can be clearly seen in the background.

Sunny Vale.

⁂

"STAFF"
Complimentary
Season Ticket.

Not Transferable.

No.......... 88

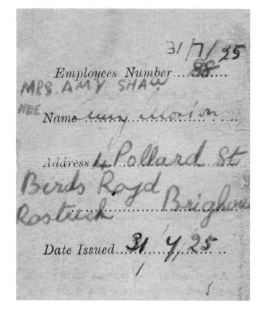

31/7/95

Employees Number.....88....

MRS. AMY SHAW

NEE *Name* Amy Morton

Address 4 Pollard St
Birds Royd
Rastrick Brighouse

Date Issued....31/7/25...

Above and below: Throughout the history of Sunny Vale many local people worked there in both a full-time capacity but predominantly as part-time seasonal staff. This staff complimentary season ticket was issued to Mrs Amy Shaw (née Morton) in 1925 and indicates that she also worked there before she was married. This staff season ticket outlines what would have been described as 'perks of the job' back in those days. I am sure that Amy and all the other employees at Sunny Vale would have been looked upon by their friends with a touch of envy, hoping that one day they too would get the opportunity of working at what was described as 'the playground of the North'.

Available for Admission any Day.

⁂

Available for Boating (per hour), One Person **6**d., Passengers **6**d. each person extra.

⁂

Rinking **6**d. per session.

⁂

Dancing Free.

⁂

Not Available for any other Amusement.

⁂

Not Available for Boating on General Holidays, or Saturdays in June, July, and August.

This Ticket will admit "Bearer" only, Friends must be paid for.

⁂

This Ticket is the Property of Messrs. Joseph Bunce & Sons, and must be given up on demand.

⁂

Employees not producing this Ticket on demand when visiting Sunny Vale, will be charged as ordinary Visitors.

⁂

Any person ceasing to be an Employee must immediately return this ticket to Joseph Bunce & Sons.

five

It's Show Time

A mesmerising performance

My earliest memories of Sunny Vale are going there with my parents when I was only four or five years old during the Second World War. We would usually go on a Bank Holiday or on a Saturday; it was always a great treat. My favourite pastime was to sit in the audience watching the concerts which were performed on a small outdoor stage which had a canopy over it in case it rained. If it did rain the audience would all dash off making for some sheltered corner — but there was always one little figure still sitting there, in the front row, mesmerised by the people performing on the stage — that was until she was forcibly removed to the same shelter by my mother!

Mrs Jean Illingworth née Martin – Hipperholme (recorded memory September 2006)

Messrs. J. BUNCE & SONS
PRESENT

MILDRED CROSSLEY

AND HER

SUNNYVALIANS

IN THE INIMITABLE ALL-STAR REVUETTE:

"Holiday Parade"

Attractive Staging —— Gorgeous Dresses
Tuneful Melodies —— Amazing Talent

Introducing the following Artistes :

CONNIE HAMER .... Versatile Tap & Acrobatic Dancer
DEREK HAMER .... The Pocket Comedian
MURIEL SWIFT .... England's own Shirley Temple
ROY CASTLE .... Wee Georgie Wood the Second
DUNCAN FLOCKHART ..... The boy with the golden voice
JOHN BROADBENT .... Our own George Formby
DOUGLAS HARRISON .... Accordionist
JOYCE LONGLEY .... Girl Soprano
JEAN PRESTON .... Child Soubrette
PHYLLIS GLEDHILL .... Tap Dancer
ELAINE MALLINSON .... Operatic Dancer
BARBARA HIGHLEY)
JEAN MIDGLEY   } .... Contortionists
DOROTHY WATERHOUSE .... Compere
MILDRED CROSSLEY, A.L.C.M. .... Pianist & Producer
OCCASIONAL GUEST ARTISTES AND
CHORUS OF INIMITABLE "VICTORY JUVENILES"

FOR DAYS AND TIMES OF PERFORMANCES—SEE BILLS
Performances will be given in the BALLROOM if wet.

J. BUNCE & SONS, SUNNY VALE, HIPPERHOLME——Tel. 69211

Singing in the rain

So it was you Jean Illingworth (née Martin) who kept us on stage in the pouring rain when everyone else had made their way to shelter under the two trees, which stood one on each side of the 'auditorium' some thirty yards away. Performing to a split audience was very tricky indeed and don't forget that we performers got wetter than the remote audience when the wind was in the wrong direction. You were blessed more than once, I can tell you. The song, 'Singing in the Rain' could well have been written especially for us. Of course in the best theatrical tradition, the show had to go on. Little did I know at the time that among the younger members of the cast was my future wife Vera (née Williamson), who remembers travelling from Elland to Sunny Vale by Mellor's taxi no less, which sounds very 'up-market' for the 1940s until you realise that there were probably twelve children packed into a six-seater with cases containing costumes and props piled on top of them. Vera and I both remember Mr Percy Bunce appearing once in a while with a tin of Smith's Crisps, remember that salt in little twists of blue paper which were, during the war years, like gold dust. It is difficult to imagine that a 2d packet of crisps would be remembered as a highlight sixty-five years later – how times have changed.
Derek and Vera Hamer, née Williamson – Brighouse (recorded memory December 2006)

1.	Opening Chorus	"We'll go Smiling Along".	
	CONCERTED		
2.	Song and Dance	Selected	
	JOYCE LONGLEY		
3.	Boy Soprano	Selected	
	DUNCAN FLOCKHART		
4.	Novelty Number	..."Paper Doll"	
	CONCERTED		
5.	Dance Solo	Tap Impressionist	
	CONNIE HAMER		
6.	Comedy and Mirth	Selected	
	DEREK HAMER		
7.	Patriotic	Tiny Tots Cabaret	
	CONCERTED		
8.	Song and a Ukelele	Selected	
	JOHN BROADBENT		
9.	Wedding Scene	"For Me and My Gal"	
	CONCERTED		
10.	Accordionist	Concerted	
	DOUGLAS HARRISON		
11.	Humorous Duet ... ..."Put your arms around me Honey"		
	MOLLIE BROADBENT, ROY CASTLE		
12.	Song and Mimic	"Pedro the Fisherman"	
	CONCERTED		
13.	Twin Contortionists	"I love to sing"	
	BARBARA HIGHLEY, JEAN MIDGLEY		
14.	Acrobatic Speciality	Selected	
	CONNIE HAMER		
15.	Wee Georgie Wood the 2nd	Selected	
	ROY CASTLE		
16.	Tap Duet	Selected	
	CONNIE and DEREK HAMER		
17.	A Military Ensemble ... "This is the Army Mr. Jones"		
	CONCERTED		
18.	Tap Duet	Selected	
	CONNIE HAMER and PAT WILKINSON		

CHANGE OF PROGRAMME AT EACH PERFORMANCE TO-DAY.

SPECIAL PERFORMANCES WITH ADDITIONAL "GUEST ARTISTES" ALL HOLIDAYS AND SPECIAL DAYS.

The songs still stick in mind

I remember being very excited when a concert party was on the stage – I watched various troupes of dancers and singers performing. Three of the songs they sang still stick in mind: 'Hey, Little Hen', 'Maisie Dotes' and 'Chicory Chick'. I can still remember the words and even have some sheet music from that time.

Mrs June Stenson – Odsal, Bradford (recorded memory August 2006)

I might have got into The Guinness Book of Records

I, along with many other children, spent most of our summer holidays performing on the open-air stage with Mildred Crossley's 'Rainbow Revels', during the whole of the Second World War years. We started our show on Good Friday every year, whatever the weather and carried on to the end of the summer holidays.

The dressing rooms were not large enough to accommodate all the performers and some of us had to change our costumes in a tent and then climb on to the stage and make our way through the wings. Roy Castle's mother was our wardrobe mistress when we did a summer season at the Queen's Theatre in Cleveleys.

One Saturday I can remember losing my purse in Huddersfield, there was about an hour and a half to go before the first performance at 3.30 p.m. and so I reckoned on it taking me half an hour to walk to Bradley Bar, half an hour into Brighouse and then a further half an hour to Sunny Vale.

Needless to say, when I arrived at the Dusty Miller there was mother waiting anxiously for me and the afternoon performance almost over. I was twelve years old. Thinking about it now if I could have walked the six and a half miles in the ninety minutes I might have got into *The Guinness Book of Records* – needless to say that was the last time mother allowed me to make my own way there.

Patricia Wimpenny, née Earnshaw – Huddersfield (recorded memory – September 1990)

PROGRAMME (continued)—

19.	Acrobatic Speciality ... ... "In a Persian Market"
	CONCERTED
20.	Six Sunbeams ... ... "Johnny's so long at the Fair"
	CONCERTED
21.	Tap Duet ... ... "Wait for me Mary"
	PHYLLIS GLEDHILL and ELAINE MALLINSON
22.	Operatic Ensemble ... ... "The Rose Ballet"
	CONCERTED
23.	The Tiny Tots entertain you in a charming number ... ...
24.	Pocket Comedian ... ... 'I'm going to get lit up"
	DEREK HAMER
25.	The Baby of the Show entertains you ... ...
	VIVIAN SPEIGHT
26.	Skipping Tap Number ... ... "Ten Little Soldiers'
	JESSIE EARNSHAW
27.	Sunbeams ... ... "Army Air Corps"
	CONCERTED
28.	Humorous ... ... "On the Banks of the Wabash"
	CONCERTED ITEM
29.	Operatic Toe Solo ... ... Selected
	CONNIE HAMER
30.	Song Scena ... ... "Down Texas Way"
	MURIEL, CONNIE and DEREK
31.	A Girl and a Piano ... ...
	MILDRED CROSSLEY—Pianist and Producer
32.	Extra.
33.	Extra.
34.	Extra.
35.	Extra. GUEST ARTISTE
36.	Grand Finale ... ... "Holiday Parade"
	FULL COMPANY

Selections from the above Programme will be presented at each Performance

Compere —— DOROTHY WATERHOUSE

It was through an advertisement in a local newspaper that a then twelve-year old Roy Castle, accompanied by his mother went to Langdale House in Elland, the home of Mildred Crossley. She ran what was then described as a dancing school-cum-concert party, which was made up of children, all of a similar age to Roy. On arrival at Langdale House, Roy and his mother were met by Mildred and shown into her studio, Roy changed into his costume which his mother had made for him especially for his audition. Roy nervously performed two pieces whilst Mildred accompanied him on the piano. She was delighted with his performance and invited him to join straight away.

Throughout the summer months Roy and his fellow performers were booked to play at Sunny Vale – here is the Alfresco Pavilion, as it was called. I had the opportunity of speaking to Roy Castle in September of 1990 about his days on the Sunny Vale stage; he recalled many happy memories.

He asked me if I knew how the Sunny Vale tea schedule worked, a question that puzzled me. He went on to explain. Visitors to Sunny Vale usually went in groups and had to pre-book their tea.

If it was a small group watching the stage performance, Hove Edge Methodists for example, they would be able to sit out on the terraced seating watching him and his friends perform on stage. If it was a bigger group, such as Brighouse Methodists, then they would have to sit on the seating and the stone steps as well. But if it was a very large group – say all the children, helpers and Sunday school teachers from the Halifax Methodist circuit – then they would have to sit on the seats, the stone steps and the surrounding grass banking along with everyone else who was watching.

This was all well and good until during one of the younger boy's first solo performances, the booming sound of 'Brighouse Methodists, your teas are ready…' echoed throughout the valley and was the cue for half the audience to suddenly get up and walk away – a very off-putting experience, particularly if it was your first time.

Me, in an undignified position

This photograph shows me in an undignified position turning round in a headstand whilst tap dancing on a round board being held by two of the boys and Betty doing the same tap steps on top of the board.
Mrs Connie Womersley, née Hamer – Lower Wyke, Bradford (recorded memory, December 2006)

A concert party on the wooden stage

I was born in Leafland Street, Halifax, I remember being taken to Sunny Vale when I was quite young, which would have been about 1926. I remember watching a concert party on the wooden stage. The men were dressed in baggy white overall trousers with red pompoms down the front, whilst the girls wore skirts and blouses. They were all wearing white shoes with pompoms and little pointed hats crowned with a pompom. I'd never seen anything like it before, as holidays were rare in those days.
Mrs Ann Fuller, née Ridsdale – Glasgow (recorded memory, September 1990)

When Roy Castle was fourteen he was given the opportunity of performing on an even bigger stage at the Queen's Theatre at Cleveleys. As the summer show at Sunny Vale was drawing to a close the theatre's owner offered Mildred two weeks in September. This was very much on a trial basis and if they were successful she would be offered a full summer season the following year. The two-week audition went very well, so well the theatre's owner Fred Thompson, who in 1946 had bought Sunny Vale and Hope Bank in Huddersfield, said he would take a chance and book them for the 1947 summer season. Roy was now on his way to eventually becoming the consummate professional performer that we all knew. Here we see Roy, all ready for another memorable performance.

On the 13 April 1995, as part of Roy's support towards his appeal to raise funds for the world's first centre of excellence in cancer research in Liverpool, he came to Halifax. This was a show at the Victoria Theatre where he was reunited with many of his old friends from the Sunny Vale days. Whilst Roy did not take part in the show he was there to support all the people who did, not just some of his old friends but the many children who took part from the numerous dancing schools and stage schools in and around the Calderdale area. Although Sunny Vale had long gone by the time this photograph was taken backstage during the show, it was a timely reminder of those happy days when they all stepped onto that wooden Alfresco Pavilion theatre stage for the first time some fifty years earlier.

Rainbow Revels, 1943: Muriel Swift, Jessie Earnshaw, Dorothy Waterhouse, Phyllis Gledhill, Connie Hamer, Miss Mildred Crossley (the dancing teacher), Derek Hamer, Pat Wilkinson, Elaine Mallinson, Dorothy Preston, Shirley Lee, Jean Preston, Mary Preston, Muriel Waterhouse, June Thorpe, Jean Midgley, Vera Williamson and Joan Earnshaw. One name missing from this group is the late Roy Castle, who appeared regularly with Mildred Crossley's 'Sunny Valians'.

Colourful crinolines

I remember quite vividly the tent (dressing room) situated at the side of the stage. The tent in question wasn't a marquee but a dome tent, which housed a least eight of us. Looking back how we ever managed so many costume changes in such a confined space – colourful dress changes which included crinolines. During the interval we had the run of the place, the skating rink being a favourite of mine but afterwards there were no showers or rest rooms. A quick wash meant soaking a hankie in the water fountains to make ourselves look presentable again.
Jean Carr, née Midgley (recorded memory, December 2006)

If you stepped out of line the discipline was strict

We had two shows on Saturday but for me it all started on Friday night. Bath, hair washed and rolled into ringlets with rags, (very uncomfortable trying to sleep with knots). Newly washed costumes had to be starched and ironed then carefully put into a suitcase with make-up and toiletries. I am sure Miss Crossley had eyes in the back of her head whilst playing the piano. She saw mistakes before they happened – if you stepped out of line (wow), the discipline was strict, but I don't think it did any of us any harm. In fact it probably helped all of us be what we are today. The comedian of the show was Tony Lester – he was funny and made everyone laugh and was very popular – little did I know at the time that twenty or so years later I would marry him.

Mrs Christine Lester, née Smith – Blackpool (recorded memory December 2006)

A nice group photograph with some of the boys and girls of the concert party with a few of the adult helpers but – oh dear – Mildred Crossley (fourth from the left) appears to be holding one of her all-too-familiar Craven A cigarettes – not the done thing today but in those days smoking by anyone was almost acceptable.

We felt like real stars

Summertime was magical; our world was lit with excitement as we spent lots of time down at Sunny Vale. At 11.30 a.m. we would go up to Mellor's garage in Elland to get the taxi which would take us all to Sunny Vale, we all felt very important arriving in a taxi, just like real stars.

Mrs Jacqueline Fisher, née Whiteley MBE (recorded memory December 2006)

Bringing the house down

Showtime – ah yes, it really was. I had a wonderful life as a child and then into my teens. I recall happy memories of Mildred Crossley, (with whom I started dancing at four and a half years old) and all 'the gang' at Sunny Vale.

I often wonder how we all managed to change in the two small dressing rooms and yet produce a smooth-running and very professional show.

There is one particular 'spot' of which I have very fond memories; that of Derek Hamer, Muriel Swift and myself, Shirley Lee (as I then was) in a comic trio of 'the Parsons of Puddle', all complete with black suits, 'dog collars' and cut-down bowler hats to make the crown about four inches deep and little wire-framed glasses on the end of our noses. Oh! Happy days, it used to bring the house down.

Shirley Crossley, née Lee (recorded memory December 2006)

An up-and-coming star

I was singing one Saturday evening at a concert at St Paul's church, Buttershaw. Mildred Crossley was also there with her concert party, the Rainbow Revels. After the concert she asked me if I would like to join them. Little did I know after a successful audition that I would be performing with an up-and-coming star like Roy Castle.

Rehearsals were every Tuesday night at her Elland studio. Each Tuesday I was given a new song to learn by the Saturday.

One Tuesday night after the rehearsal I came out to catch the bus but owing to the fog it had been cancelled, so I walked to Halifax (five miles) with the intention of then walking to my home in Wibsey (six and a half miles). Thankfully, I was given a lift home by someone in one of the few cars about in those days. On arrival at home my parents were in a state of near panic, not knowing where I was – no mobile phones in those days.

When Mildred Crossley went to Cleveleys I had to drop out to carry on with my apprenticeship.

In 1995 I went to the Victoria Theatre in Halifax to support Roy Castle and his charity. To meet Roy and many of the former members of Mildred's concert party was certainly a memorable experience after fifty years.

Eric Fawthrop – Lightcliffe (recorded memory December 2006)

Best of all, Roy Castle had marmite with us

After all the shows we used to dash to the skating rinks, rowing on the boats and playing in the Penny Arcade.

We had to go to the tea rooms where we were given just bread and butter (margarine) and one plain bun. We soon all started taking our own things for sandwiches, such as jam, marmalade but best of all was marmite, which Roy Castle had with us as well

Mrs Phyllis Smith, née Gledhill (recorded memory December 2006)

The Sunny Vale Perriots performing on the Alfresco Pavilion theatre stage during the 1930s.

Travelling to Mildred Crossley's

In 1939 I was fourteen and was invited to join Mildred Crossley's concert party. Every Wednesday we had to attend rehearsals at her home in Elland. On concert days (Saturdays) I had to get a trolley bus from Lockwood in Huddersfield. Also travelling to Sunny Vale was a gymnast called Jack Norman who lived at The Slades in Linthwaite. There was also a girl singer who I believe was called Sylvia Stockdale, when she was older she started singing with the 'Big Bands' who were performing in and around the Huddersfield area at the time.

Geoff Dyson – Milnsbridge, Huddersfield (recorded memory September 2006)

Mildred Crossley

Mildred Crossley is pictured below in the early 1940s (centre, front row), taking time out with parents of some of the children in her Sunny Vale concert party. Mildred Crossley was born in Elland and made her first stage appearance at the tender age of four. From then on she performed regularly both as a singer and a dancer. She went on to study the piano and soon passed her examinations. She finished her grammar school education at sixteen and took up a musical career straightaway. She formed a school of stage training and music which soon became very well known and practically a household word in the West Riding area of Yorkshire. In time this school became known as MC Productions, Langdale House, Langdale Street, Elland. Hundreds of successful pupils passed through her training school having been taught piano, music and dancing, examinations and degrees. She also produced many young star performers who went on to become professional dancers and entertainers. During her career she also produced many semi-professional and professional revues, sketches and solos from these shows, being her own original ideas. Amongst these shows were 'Cruising the World', 'The Coronation Revue', 'Youth on Parade', 'Youth Takes a Bow', 'The Rainbow Revels' and one of her most successful

shows, 'Happiness Ahead'. In addition to these shows she also wrote various pantomimes. Many times she was referred to as one of the finest female producers in the country. Visitors to her Elland studios or the Alfresco Pavilion at Sunny Vale or the Queens Theatre in Cleveleys would often be heard to comment about her unbounded enthusiasm and the personality of every artiste, large or small, and their likeness was often compared to that of a large family. She was credited with the same enthusiasm and personality which she instilled into each and every one of her young performers. In addition to being recognised as a tremendous show producer she was also considered to be a very fine pianist and artistes would often comment on her excellent skills as an accompanist. In 1940 she married Norman Teal, a professional xylophonist with Herman Darewski and his orchestra. On occasions, he too appeared at Sunny Vale – as a couple they were recognised as being the youngest revue producer-owners in the country. They had one daughter, Maureen, who by the age of six was showing signs of having inherited her parents' love of the stage and was also a fine pianist.

The end of an era

When I was nineteen (back row, third from the left), I took over the Sunny Vale shows on Saturdays for Mildred Crossley with the boys and girls who, like me, preferred to stay at home. However, after the war was over the crowds who had loved to visit Sunny Vale were now able to get petrol for their cars again and set off to the coast for their holidays – the end of an era.

Connie Womersley, née Hamer - Lower Wyke (recorded memory December 2006)

We got to know those slot machines very well

I started going to Mildred Crossley's dancing school in the mid-1940s when Sunny Vale Pleasure Gardens was a very popular spot. Every summer weekend Miss Crossley (as we all had to call her) used to put on her concerts at the open-air theatre there. The lay of the land lent itself very nicely as the stage was at the bottom of a gentle slope with the seating extending upwards to where there was a café at the top. They were very happy times as we all loved to dance. My dancing partner was a boy called David Hancock; I wonder where he is now. We were picked up by a coach and taken to Sunny Vale with our costumes, tap and ballet shoes and the all-important packed lunch to sustain us between shows; not to mention a quick prayer for fine weather. As far as I can remember there were only two dressing rooms, situated one either side of the stage; girls one side and boys the other. The concerts were full of a variety of talent and Miss Crossley ruled us with a rod of iron, woe betide anyone who put a foot wrong during a performance. There was a roller-skating rink and penny slot machines which we took advantage of during the break. We got to know those slot machines very well, especially the ones that paid out most often. I am sat on the front row wearing the white ankle socks.

Vera Kerridge, née Shaw – Sowerby (recorded memory December 2006)

Eric Martin, son of a prominent Bradford coal merchant, became the Bradford theatre producer who had taken a lease on Sunny Vale in 1952 from Fred Thompson but within twelve months he gave up the lease. Eric ran the old Bradford Mechanics' Institute as a music hall between 1941 and 1947 and made many discoveries. Perhaps his greatest find was Harry Worth who he put on the stage at the Mechanics' in June 1946 and then gave a chance to the boy comedian from Huddersfield – Roy Castle. He also discovered the world-famous hypnotist Peter Casson. Eric Martin also arranged the 'Stay at Home' holiday entertainments in Bradford Parks. He was also responsible for giving Winifred Atwell her chance. Eric, the Bradford theatre impresario, died in 1984.

Mildred Crossley was not the only person who had young stage performers at Sunny Vale:

In Clifton village on the outskirts of Brighouse Ernest and Mary Hudson decided to put together a children's concert party. We were all from the local Methodist Sunday school and called 'the Victory Follies'. We performed regularly at Sunny Vale, as well as other communities in the West Riding. But Sunny Bunces was our favourite. This photograph was taken at the Cosmo Studios in Brighouse in 1943 and shows just a few of the members. From left to right: Ronnie Davison, Sheila Crowther, Anne Shirley Pratt, Cynthia Shaw, Kathleen Bray, Doreen Shaw and Peter Greenwood.

Peter Greenwood – Hightown (recorded memory September 2006)

This 1943 photograph of 'the Victory Follies' was taken at the back of the parish hall in Church Lane, Brighouse. Members of the concert party here include: Sheila Conway, Mavis Marshall, Doreen Shaw, Kathleen Crowther, Ronnie Davison, Peter Greenwood, Joan Robinson, Joan Dilley, Trevor Nicholson, Joyce Nicholson, Marlene Rathmell, V: unknown, I: Sheila Crowther, T: Pat Robinson, O: Maureen Conway, R: unknown and Y: Denise Hudson. Other regular cast members who are absent included: Jean Walker, Gwen Thornton, Christine Womersley, Margaret Clay, Valerie Bennett, Mavis Hookham, Arnold Burkett and Alan Whittaker. The choreographer was Kathleen Hobson; the writer and producer was Dennis Brewer and the pianist was Peter Greenwood.

A dress rehearsal

When I was fourteen going on fifteen, I appeared on the stage at Sunny Vale myself with the Brighouse Follies. At Easter time we used to do a show there, I remember one particular Easter it was snowing and so we did the show in the tea rooms instead. There was a stage in there, I don't think we had anyone in the audience, apart from a few ladies who had come to help with the costumes, but we didn't care; we just did the show as a dress rehearsal.

Miss Beverley Holmes – Bailiff Bridge (recorded memory December 2006)

six

Trains, Boats and Donkeys

Throughout Sunny Vale children had the opportunity of riding on all kinds of transport and not just on a boat either, as we will soon see. To a child of four going on five, those long hot summers during the early 1940s were a million miles away from the problems of war-torn Europe.

The day dad fell in the lake

Sometimes, if it was a bank holiday there would be a Punch and Judy show which all the children loved. Back in those days no one bothered whether it was politically correct or not – it was funny. At the end of a lovely afternoon out it usually came to an end with a trip on one of the lakes in a rowing boat with dad puffing and blowing as he rowed us round and round the islands. I will never forget the day he fell in. As everyone stepped out of the boat from one end which left dad at the other end of the boat on his own, it suddenly tipped up with dad still in it. I started to cry – not because dad was in the water, he could swim – but he still had my toffees in his pocket. I'm glad to say dad was okay and so were my toffees – once his suit had dried and had been cleaned it looked brand new.
Jean Illingworth, née Martin – Chesterfield (recorded memory September 2006)

Gliding along on a suspended chair – I wasn't sure whether I dreamt it all!

I remember Sunny Vale from the late 1940s and '50s back in the days when I lived in Norwood Green and we would be taken on a Sunday school outing from St George's church in Village Street. We used to meet for Sunday school in the Mission Room which in those days was next to the 'Lane Ends Inn' public house, in Village Street (which has long since closed down). We walked down to Norwood Green Railway Station, two by two, hand in hand, in snake fashion. We caught the train to Hipperholme. In those days for us it was quite a novelty to go on a train – still in the days of 'steam'. A little group of us – the Pinders, Ramsdens, and Marshalls, plus two others – enjoyed a compartment in the carriage all to ourselves, so there was no communication with the rest of the party until we alighted. We were all between eight and eleven years old; it was great fun… At Sunny Vale I can remember the steep slope down leading to a boating lake. At the bottom we eventually met for our afternoon tea down here. Down the slope as far as I remember were slides with slight undulations on them, but the feature I liked was at the top. It was a chair suspended from an overhead oblong track which one glided along. But every now and then there was a dip in the track which caused the chair to swing forwards and back. I simply loved being on it and spent most of my time there. I went back some years later and there seemed to be no evidence of all the fun things that were there – I wasn't sure whether I dreamt it all!
Katherine Ching, née Marshall – Ripon (recorded memory October 2006)

Pony and donkey rides were always a real treat for the thousands of visiting children. Throughout the summer months those ponies and donkeys would have to work tirelessly for all those children who, in many cases, had probably never seen one close up before.

Decorated carts and lovely horses

I visited Sunny Vale several times, we always called it Sunny Bunces – of course it was a very happy day out, lots of children and parents, usually on Sunday school outings. There were decorated carts and lovely horses all beautifully groomed and trimmed with ribbon. We had wonderful teas all spread out and all homemade with every sort of sandwich and cake you could think of. We rode on carts and ran in races and had a wonderful day and finished it off singing hymns. I would have been about twelve years old then, during the early 1920s.
Mrs R. Pearson – Fulford, York (recorded memory August 1990)

The Sunny Vale Horse Keeper

For many years my dad Willie Kershaw looked after the boating rides on the big lake at Sunny Vale. He was a friend of Tommy Womersley, who was the donkey man or, as he liked to be called, 'the Horse Keeper' at Sunny Vale. In those days there were eight to ten donkeys and a couple of Shetland ponies. Those donkeys and ponies never stopped working throughout the season – they were a real favourite with all the children. Dad started working there in 1921 on a part-time basis at weekends and holiday times. He often told me about the special trains that came to Hipperholme Station from Barnsley and places in Lancashire. During the 1930s he got a promotion – up from the donkeys to the Helter-Skelter and the swings, rotating from one to the other with another of the part-timers. Dad worked there until the war started in 1939.

Norman Kershaw – Brighouse (recorded memory November 2006)

The children were rather special with fathers abroad

During the war years, in approximately 1943, during the summer months, parties of children were taken to Sunny Vale on Halifax Corporation buses, leaving from Thornton Square in Brighouse, where we lived at that time. The children were rather special because their fathers were abroad with the armed services. The treat I suspect was arranged possibly by the British Legion, although I am not certain.

On arrival at Sunny Vale we were given tickets for the train ride, the boats and for what seemed enormous at the time: a huge slide. We were taken to an open-air theatre to see the Punch and Judy show, some singers and clowns. After the treat we were then taken to the cafeteria which overlooked the amusement park for our tea.

Ron Broadbent – Keighley (recorded memory September 1990)

Before the arrival of the Bassett-Lowke 'Little Giant' 15-inch miniature railway in 1923, the nearest visitors came to riding a train was a switchback ride which was in use as early as 1895. Here is the downward track of the switchback ride which ran in front of the tea rooms.

This image of the early switchback ride in front of the tea room is taken from publicity material Joseph Bunce used to promote his pleasure gardens.

This extremely rare, 1895 image of the switchback ride is at the top of the run. The man at the front would have been the brake man. The paying public riding this for the first time would have never experienced anything like it before and it must have been exhilarating, as well as scary.

The switchback ride made its way down the track with the children screaming with delight and the ladies keeping a tight hold of their hats as the wind whistled passed them. Pedestrians walking down from the tea rooms to this crossing point would have had to keep a sharp eye out and listen out for the switchback ride as it approached and trundled passed them.

In 1922 Lionne Bunce, the daughter of James Farnell Bunce, was born – an event that was a joy in itself but also one that would be embedded in the annals of Sunny Vale forever. By way of celebrating her birth the family named Sunny Vale's new miniature train 'Baby Bunce' after her. Here we see carriages packed with visitors enjoying the sights and sounds from the more controlled and comfortable seating offered on the new train rather than what had previously been on offer with the old switchback ride.

The 'Baby Bunce' miniature railway is still remembered today by many of the people who visited Sunny Vale. The train, a Bassett-Lowke Ltd class 10, 15-inch Little Giant miniature railway, was first seen by the general public at the Blackpool Pleasure Beach between 1905 and 1909. At Blackpool the train originally went on a circular route round a gipsy encampment and pulled into a small railway station which the owners called 'Gipsyville'. This small complex situated on the south shore was destined for a big future. It wasn't until 1906 that it was renamed as the more familiar Blackpool Pleasure Beach. In 1909, Little Giant was on its way to Halifax Zoo and Amusement Park at Chevinedge, between Elland and Siddal on the outskirts of Halifax, which opened in 1910. After the zoo closed in 1916 and the amusement park the following year through the difficulties of the First World War the train was placed in storage. In 1922 it was being offered for sale in a copy of the *Model Engineer* magazine.

Sunny Vale had been in operation just over forty years by the time 'Baby Bunce' was up and running. Sadly it was not to last; in 1946, having made the decision to sell, the whole site and all its contents were sold as previously indicated. Despite the owners' efforts, by the late forties, Sunny Vale was a shadow of its former self and a pretty tired one at that. The place was put up for sale in 1949 but there were no bids. In 1952 Eric Martin, a theatrical producer from Bradford, took it on but he faired no better. The following year D. & J. MacNulty, two brothers from Morecambe, tried to make a go of it, but the life of Sunny Vale was now coming to an end. In 1955 Fred Thompson sold off the contents and then in 1958 placed the whole place up for auction once again and this time everything was sold off.

When Sunny Vale closed, 'Baby Bunce' was bought by a dealer in Bishop Auckland who renamed it 'Robin Hood' and later sold it to a fairground in the Newcastle area. That was a failure because the owners found it was too big to run at the fairground, so once again it was placed in storage. It was then sold again. Whilst being restored, the initials SVMR (Sunny Vale Miniature Railway) were discovered and the owner realised that he had the 'Little Giant' on his hands. Reverting back to its original name it was then purchased by John Henderson, a rail enthusiast. From 1981 'Little Giant' was at Lightwater Valley as well as at Ravenglass in Cumbria where once again it was thrilling young children with every ride it gave.

After extensive enquires I am now informed that 'Little Giant' is on a period of loan to the National Railway Museum at York and can be seen in the museum's Great Hall.

Outside the Travellers public house in 1933. Left to right: Marjorie Wood, Doreen Wood, May Sherwood, Gracie Hewitt, Carl Towl, Dorothy Ward and Tommy Daw. All these children lived in Station Hill or Tanhouse Hill.

Bye Bye Blackbird

I was born Doreen Wood, the youngest of six children, in 1926 at 3 Station Road (aka 3 Tanhouse Hill), Hipperholme. It is on the corner. We moved to 4 Tanhouse Hill in about 1942, where I lived until I married in 1947. My grandfather Frank Wood lived at Change View, just up the road. It was about ten minutes' walk to 'Bunces', as we called it, so we went there often. That was when we had the pennies to do so. I think it cost about 2d for adults and 1d for children, perhaps more at holidays and at weekends. You entered by the turnstiles – sometimes we sneaked in around the back, it was horrible round there, loads of frogs and they would jump up at your legs.

Bus trips used to come and park opposite our house and the people would walk down Station Hill into the valley and they would also come by train. Everyone would be dressed up in their Sunday best. It was very busy with crowds of people, families mainly. When they were leaving lots of people went to the Travellers pub, people would also knock on our door and ask for a drink of water. We always made sure we had jugs filled ready. We thought this was great as kids! People would stand outside the pub drinking, it was a busy pub at that time – the Towls had the pub then.

There used to be an old man with one leg, who played what I would call a barrel organ which he would carry over his shoulder. He would sit at the top of Station Hill on the pavement turning it to play 'Bye Bye Blackbird'. We used to sit on the wall at the entrance to the track that went up to the delve to watch him, but he used to tell us to clear off and send us away. I must have been about ten years old then. People would throw money into his cap – we called him Bye Bye Blackbird as this was what he always played. He would then go to the Travellers. I don't know if he changed his pennies or spent them.

From being about seven years old I can remember going down to Bunces. I remember two lakes; the larger one had an island in the middle and there were rowing boats. There was a walkway and grassed area where people sat or laid about. On the other side of the lake ran the Baby Bunce train, 2d return or 1d one way. I once got off on the island and then had to wait for my friends to come back and rescue me! In winter the lake would ice over and was used for ice-skating. I couldn't afford ice-skates but my sister Hilda had some. The other lake had paddle boats on it.

There used to be a slide, you could sit on chairs and ride it to the top for 2d – mind you, it was only a penny if you walked! There was an arcade with slot machines and a *What the Butler Saw*-type viewing machine. I remember an electric-shock machine; we would stand in a row holding each others' hand to feel the shock go through all of us! There was also a Hall of Mirrors that made you look thin and fat. Outside was a spice stall selling acid drops, bulls' eyes and toffee lollipops. There were Swing Boats – I used to like those and a Maze where we played hide and seek.

At holiday times and at weekends, different brass bands would play in the bandstand. There was an area for dancing or you sat and just watched nearby. There was a roller-skating rink – you could hire skates and go skating for 6d. There was only one friend that I remember having her own skates and she lived in the grounds of Bunces. I believe her family had something to do with the tea rooms. We never used to go there but they always appeared to be busy. Not far away was an outdoor stage where shows were put on, with dancing and a pierrot and my cousin Bobby played the accordion.

Doreen Evans, née Wood – Doncaster (recorded memory September 2006)

Above, left and right: These two items were promotional gifts that could be either bought or won from one of the sideshows. Even after all these years since the closure of Sunny Vale, items of nostalgia such as these can be found at car boot sales and antiques fairs.

It is many years since Sunny Vale last saw the vast crowds of children pouring down the narrow lane to make sure they didn't miss out on any of the excitement. Since those heady days the land has been excavated, raced on, tipped on, gardened and after all that just occasionally, an old piece of Sunny Vale nostalgia is unearthed.

This old sweet tin – well, what there is left of it now – was one supplied by Charles W. Mattock Ltd, a manufacturing confectioners from Sowerby Bridge, who used to sell toffee. The Bunce family had these special tins manufactured as a promotional item.

seven

And There
Was More

To gain legitimate access into Sunny Vale all visitors had to go in via one of the turnstiles. However, there were a number of, let us say, unofficial ways in. From all my enquiries it would seem these unofficial access points were known by all the local children, in particular those living in Southowram. This waterfall was at the back of the amusement park in an area known as Pinnell Bridge. Once you were across this small rickety old bridge which led through to the back of the Maze, many local children knew exactly where the fence was at its weakest and they could sneak in for nothing.

A piece of priceless knowledge

My memory takes me back to 1944 and our gang. We would roly-poly down the fields to Sunny Vale. The older members of our gang knew where the holes were in the hedge – a piece of priceless knowledge that was passed down to you as you got older. We squeezed through the hedge and bushes and suddenly you found yourself in the Maze.

Marlene Ward, née Shackleton - Southowram (recorded memory September 2006)

Through the secret entrance

My most vivid memory of Sunny Vale is of a visit probably when I was twelve in 1950. I spent all my available money on the Glacier slide. It was a tremendous affair compared to the normal playground slide.

I lived in Finkil Street, Hove Edge and together with Jimmy Farrar and Chris Greaves we played a great deal of our time in the valley from ages nine to fourteen, mainly near the stream and used to go into Sunny Vale via the 'free' entrance to catch sticklebacks in the lower lake. I seem to recall that this secret entrance that all the local children our age knew about was at the corner of the lake near the stream bridge rather than the one behind the Maze.

I remember just after the war – that Easter Monday was a very popular day – rumours of up to 20,000 visitors and a huge firework display – what a time we had.

Geoff Hopkinson – Beaconsfield, Buckinghamshire (recorded memory October 2006)

Affectionately known as Bunces

I am seventy-six years old and well remember Sunny Vale which was affectionately known as 'Bunces', both my parents worked there and a large part of my childhood was spent there roller-skating and rowing the boats. My dad helped to make the Maze.

Mrs N. Grime – Shaw, Greater Manchester (recorded memory August 1990)

Here we see what is described as 'a corner of the Maze'. Trying to establish just when the Maze was created is very difficult but the only available records would certainly indicate it was pre-1907. However, Lionne Crossley, the granddaughter of Joseph Bunce suggests that the Maze was part of the original pleasure gardens which pre-dated the amusement park. She also points out that the shape of the Maze was based on the maze at Hampton Court, the royal palace on the Thames to the west of London which is probably the most famous hedge maze in the world.

Comparing this photograph with the earlier one above, it is clear to see there has been quite a bit of tidying up done by the gardeners. We can see the ladies standing on the gantry: it was from this vantage point that these ladies and other parents could keep an eye on their children as they all got lost in the Maze and inevitably became upset. Many other children would cross this bridge and instead of walking over the gantry they would manage to climb through a loose part of the fence and then find themselves in the Maze. All they had to do then was to negotiate their way out of the Maze and then they were home and dry, they too could join all their friends who had once again successfully got into Sunny Bunces free of charge.

During the late 1940s the Maze was in a poor state of repair. Some former visitors have even said that by that time you could almost see through the hedge Maze from one side to the other. William Henley, who had been involved in planting the Maze at the end of the nineteenth century, would have been greatly saddened to see how much it had been allowed to deteriorate. It was clear that after the departure of the Bunce family, everything they had worked for and had very successfully created over sixty years was rapidly coming to an end.

Try and picture the scene – youngsters manage to get in through the fence on the right-hand side, then stand in the Maze crying to attract the attention of a man who worked on the gantry looking out for distressed children. He would hear the children crying and rush down to help them, escorting them into the park and then the children would promptly run off in the crowds and yes, you have guessed it, that was two more youngsters who had managed to get in for free.

The frog was warning us of impending doom

In the valley at Hove Edge was a place called Sunny Vale or, as we called it, 'Sunny Bunces'. I think the chap who started it must have been called Mr Bunce. Whether his disposition was sunny I don't know. Sunny Bunces was what was then called an inland resort. During the war you couldn't get to the seaside so places like Sunny Vale and over in Huddersfield, 'Hope Valley', were set up. All are gone now. History is now repeating itself and inland resorts are coming back: Lightwater Valley, Alton Towers etc. I hope this doesn't bode evil.

'Sunny Vale' had two boating lakes, a scenic railway, and a proper hedge maze with a wooden tower in the middle to spot lost folk from and lots of fairground attractions. Sunday school trips went there and you were let loose on the site with a yard of paper tickets to go on the rides. My first boat trip was there. Dad took me out on the lake in a small pedalo boat. It was terrifying; the boat had a list to one side, so one revolving paddle splashed almost out of the water. So, we tried to compensate by leaning to one side. The boat was awash; I thought from the start we were going to sink.

We set off, dad pedalling; we travelled in an arc to the middle of the lake. My feet were getting wet. I looked down at the water in the boat bottom. A large frog had appeared as if to see what was going on and if perhaps we were going his way. He wasn't there when we set off and I hadn't seen him jump in so I instantly assumed he must have got on board through a hole in the bottom of the boat… this confirmed in my mind that we were going to sink. I knew holes in boats didn't let water out and I hadn't got my swimming certificate yet. A return to dry land as quick as possible seemed in order, which I tried to indicate to dad by waving my arms, pointing at the frog and the shore. Dad being a countryman couldn't understand why I appeared to be so scared of a frog and why I wanted to take it back to land. He smiled and nodded in the direction of the frog as if to say, 'it's okay – frogs can swim'.

I looked down, the frog had gone. This was worse; the frog had abandoned ship, probably back through the same hole he'd come by. The frog had gone, he knew we were sinking. Dad was determined to get his money's worth and carried on casually peddling and paddling. When the water started washing the fluff and bus tickets out of his trouser turn-ups he realised we were actually slowly sinking. Then his heroic efforts to get to the bank were sight to behold. The paddle sticking out of the water made us go in circles but we made it before the boat sank. The frog was nowhere to be seen. He'd done his job warning us of impending doom, like the dolphins saving men at sea.

Wilf Lunn – Huddersfield (an extract from Chapter 13, 'Laikin' of his autobiography, for further reading please see www.wilflunn.com)

The Automatic Café – no staff required. This would have seemed a very strange concept in the 1930s, long before the days of self-service or the coffee bar or the milk bar of the 1950s. The management at Sunny Vale were certainly ahead of their time with this catering facility. Just when it was first introduced as a new facility for the visitors is as yet unknown. It might have been from here where those who considered themselves 'posh' might have sat in the chairs provided and looked on, watching and listening to the sights and sounds across the lake. Whilst everyone else would have had to settle for just a covered area where small children could tuck into home-made doorstep sandwiches.

The main tea room was at the top of the gardens and had been the original farmhouse. It had a mains water supply, reasonable toilet facilities and all the required comforts including sweet-smelling soap. For those at the bottom of the gardens there were open closets with the liquid waste running out into the beck, which flowed past the back of the Maze. With that thought in mind, you now have to think about the largest gathering ever recorded at Sunny Vale over a four-day Bank Holiday period – 52,500. Now consider the toilet facilities – oh dear – and then the children who used to swim in the same beck about a mile downstream. It does not bear thinking about.

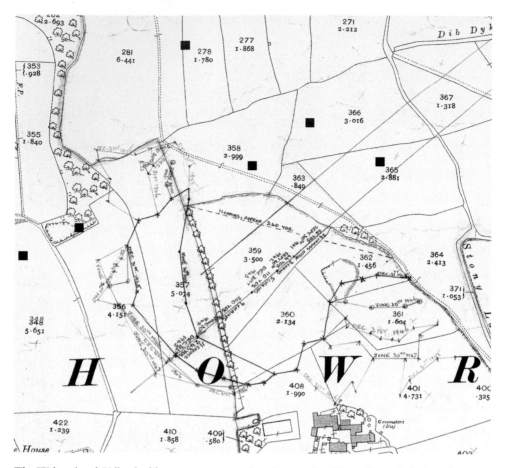

The Walterclough Valley had become accustomed to the sounds of Percy Bunce's choice of music to entertain the visitors: Gilbert and Sullivan, *The Maid of the Mountains*, *Florrie Forde's Favourites* and music from the shows which included *The New Moon* and *The Belle of New York*. These were the sounds that echoed throughout the valley for six months of the year, along with the strains of many a brass band performing week-in, week-out on the bandstand.

In August of 1940, however, there were sounds of a very different kind when the Second World War literally landed on the doorstep of this small community. It was on the night of Saturday 24 August 1940 with weather reports showing it was cloudy throughout the North of England and responding to the sound of aircraft high above Hove Edge. The searchlight battery placement in a field on Halifax Road was showing a full beam, along with a number of other searchlights, and they were soon converging on the sound of German aircraft.

One German bomber was picked up in the shafts of light that penetrated the night sky – the pilot, with a full load of six bombs, was determined not to be shot down whilst still carrying his deadly cargo. He veered off sharply out of the column of light as he flew over the Walterclough Valley and there, in a desperate attempt to escape, he dumped his six-bomb load into the valley bottom. That action thankfully resulted in no fatalities, although one lady with the shock did fall down the stairs in her cottage and break her leg.

The following day, spectators arrived in their droves and it was reported that local children had a field day looking for shrapnel to swap and show off to their friends. I have an old ordnance survey map that once belonged to the Brookes Stone Co., who owned a significant amount of land in the valley. Someone at the company has carefully marked the sites where the six bombs landed.

eight

Winter Work

Sunny Vale employed as many as forty people after the main summer season was over – some would be painting and putting the rides away until next season. This was something that never happened after the Bunce family sold it. Some of the people employed during the winter time were involved in making holly wreaths and other Christmas decorations. Fred Thompson had bought the Sunny Vale Pleasure Gardens site on 1 July 1946 but even after leasing the site out, firstly to Eric Martin in May 1952 and then to D. & J. MacNulty, two brothers from Morecambe in March 1953 – the end had finally come and the Sunny Vale that countless visitors had enjoyed was to close. The contents were sold off at public auction and then in May of 1958 the site was bought by Mr Herbert (Bert) Myers and his wife Alice. On the property deeds Bert is described as a retired master builder from Northwich in Cheshire. It was Mr and Mrs Myers who initially decided to update the name with something that might have been considered by its potential new members as being a little more sophisticated, 'the Sunny Vale Country Club'. This was all part of their new £20,000 planned improvement scheme, which was to be implemented as the new club prospered, with a camping and caravan park planned to enhance the facilities. It was anticipated that the new club would generate a membership of 500, with each new member paying an annual fee of ten shillings; these fees would finance the ongoing improvements. However, the local newspapers reported that the idea only attracted seventy-five paid-up members. The late Sir Donald Thompson who grew up in the Hipperholme and Lightcliffe areas and in his later years was the Member of Parliament for the district told me that he was one of the few young people to join the new club. Sadly as he recalled, 'they were never going to be able to make a go of Sunny Vale again, certainly not in the way that everyone remembered it as from the old days.' But even as it struggled Sunny Vale still had a few visitors, some of whom even ventured out on a boat. However, the world was changing. The Second World War changed many things; people's expectations were far higher and some were financially better off than the generations before. The owners of the Sunny Vale Country Club realised something new had to be found and found quickly…

A great day paddling round the lake

In the late 1940s or early '50s, I was working at Grysdale's (F. Barraclough & Co.), who were funeral directors in Lightcliffe Road, Brighouse. The Bunce family sold the park in 1946 and the new owners who bought the place were proposing to do it up. During the bad winter of 1947 George Bottomley, Peter Pettrick (who lived at Hipperholme), Douglas Eccles and I were taken down to Bunces and as well as having to do a lot of repairs to the huts, fences and such like we also had the job of lifting out all the tin paddle boats from the bottom of the lake, for possible re-use. Whilst lifting the boats out I remember Lionne Bunce watching us while she was out walking and to both her and our amusement Douglas Eccles fell in, mind you I think we all got a little wet that day, larking about. The boats had been sunk by kids and we had a great day paddling round that lake.
Philip Helme – Yarm, North Yorkshire (recorded memory December 2006)

My parents Fred and Ivy King came to Sunny Vale from Huntingdon *c.* 1930 and they were the caretakers for about thirty years. My father looked after Kitty the carthorse and most of the amusements. My Aunt Ada Risely had moved to Sunny Vale twelve months before us and was the manageress of the tea rooms until they sold out to the Thompsons.

Ivy, Mrs Coleman and Mrs Ripley were all waitresses in the tea rooms which were very busy in the summer months. The winter, however, was rather desolate unless it was a bad cold snap when the lakes were frozen over and ice-skating was on. I remember my father hosing it at night for an extra layer of ice – my sister was quite a good skater. We couldn't wait until Good Friday when everything opened up for the new season.

During the pre-Christmas period my mother, auntie and others made holly wreaths which were sold at local markets. I had a favourite rowing boat and when they were not fit to use anymore they were cut in half and made into sheltered seats around the bottom lake and were good courting places. I remember Mildred Crossley and her dancing troupe where my sisters and I had a sneaky try of some of the costumes.

Being there so long we could walk round the Maze without coming to a dead end. After the Thompsons came we moved out.

Doreen (Dolly) Maude, née King – Southowram (recorded memory December 2006)

An enterprising nature

[A name synonymous with Sunny Vale and the local community was that of Ripley's Ice Cream]. Fred Ripley was my uncle – as a young man he served his time as an apprentice engineer but there was no job at the end of his time. He was a talented violinist and played in the silent cinema. He probably started on the ice cream around 1930. The dairy and stables were at the junction of Half House Lane and Wood Bottom Lane. There were three carts and the stall at Sunny Vale, my mother worked there at holiday times. With the coming of the sugar rationing he still managed to make ice cream but it was only a fraction of his pre-war production. The stables were closed and the horses were sold off – he now turned his enterprising nature back to his first job, that of an engineer working from his own workshop which housed about half a dozen working lathes.

His sister Anne and my cousin Mary pretty well worked full-time for him but he also employed no end of other people on a part-time basis. It was repetitive work; he just had to keep a check on the stuff they turned out, they machined Woodcock and Booth castings. This work came to an end with the end of the war. After the war I believe he had just one van for ice cream but he had a choc-ice machine. He sold the choc-ices to direct retail outlets.

During the early 1950s he had two bungalows built in Vicarage Road, Marton near Blackpool. He lived in one of them and my cousin Mary and her husband George Hanson in the other. George was a well known saxophone player in the pre-war years in Brighouse.

Ted Murray – West Bromwich (recorded memory December 2006)

Above: During the school holidays many local children worked at Sunny Vale particularly in the winter months. Here the children are helping to prepare Christmas trees ready for sale in local markets.

Here are two people who worked at Sunny Vale during the winter months. Although I have searched for many years and can name the young man as Charlie Gomersal, I still cannot give a name to the young lady other than perhaps the mistletoe tester!

The Lightwater Valley of yesterday

My mother worked in the tea rooms at the top of the gardens – this was opposite the theatre where Mildred Crossley ran her talent contests and shows. Incidentally it was also where Roy Castle started. My brother Dennis used to work in the Automatic Café which was down at the bottom by the lake.

The tea rooms served ham or corned beef salads, tea, bread and butter and when it was busy my friend and I used to go down and serve. Quite a few ladies worked in the kitchen preparing; one of them was my auntie.

As it was rationing time and because it was a café they got coupons for bread, butter and other things. Cups of tea were sold to those people who brought their own food. Visitors to Sunny Vale came from all over Yorkshire and Lancashire, even though they had Belle Vue on their doorstep. Sunny Vale was like the Lightwater Valley of today. It really was a wonderful place. Children didn't wonder what to do with their time because they could always go down to Bunces.

The amusements included a Helter-Skelter ride and a ride at the top which ran on rails which dipped down in places – later on they had dodgems and many more. I remember the lake being frozen over in 1947/48 and it was crowded with skaters. Baby Bunce was the name of their miniature railway which ran around the top lake – I remember the driver was called John Holmes and he lived in Hove Edge.

Mrs Joyce McAdam, née Bottomley (recorded memory December 2006)

nine

Beginning
of the End

When I worked on the rink

Sunny Vale roller-skating rink and four good friends, *c.* 1954. From left to right: Terry Womersley, Selwyn Green, Sidney Spalding and David Beverley. The rink at that time was leased by Peter Green, who had a greengrocer's shop at Rastrick and was Selwyn's brother. It was a great place to go in the evenings and weekends. The skating rink lighting was run from a diesel generator. Quite often the generator would cut out and the whole place was suddenly thrown into darkness with the inevitable bumpity-bump as the skaters knocked each other over. There was not much left of the old Sunny Vale apart from the roller-skating rink and the boats when I worked on the rink. In those days the main turnstiles to enter the Sunny Vale site although still in place were no longer used. There was a turnstile to go on the skating rink and it was that turnstile that I was in charge of. In the old tea rooms there was a youth club which attracted youngsters from as far away as Halifax. Sometime about 1958 the rink was closed down, leaving the youth club to carry on for a few more years. I had been going to Sunny Vale from when I was a child after the war until I was married.

Sidney Spalding – Lightcliffe (recorded memory December 2006)

My first meeting with Joyce

I was working on the roller-skating rink when in 1956 two girls came to the rink. As they had no money I would not let them go on for free. Later that evening they returned with some money and enjoyed themselves roller-skating. One of these girls was Joyce Kidman; not long after that first meeting she and I started going out together and then in the early 1960s we got married. This photograph shows Joyce and me on one of the boats and was taken during the summer. It was not long after we were married that we stopped going to Sunny Vale.

Sidney and Joyce (née Kidman) Spalding – Lightcliffe (recorded memory December 2006)

The owners of Sunny Vale certainly started something when the Go-Karting was in full swing. Whilst it attracted large crowds of enthusiasts it was also the start of problems for the residents who lived in the valley. These are some of the prime movers of the Go-Karting era. Back row (from left to right): one of the Shaw twins, Ronnie Cowgill, the other Shaw twin and Alan Parks. Front row: Frank Staples, Laurie Morgan, Bill Craythorne, Eddie Orton and Ron Smith. This photograph was taken in 1962 at the Bankfield Hotel, Bradford on the occasion of the annual dinner.

Budding F1 racers at Sunny Vale

I have many happy memories of Sunny Vale back in the sixties. The Go-Karting track was originally laid as a rather tough tarmacadam surface which was dug out of the hillside by Ronnie Cowgill, who was tragically killed in 1965. Ronnie's partner in laying the track was Bill Craythorne. There was another person involved called Ron Smith, who came from Odsal.

At a later date the surface was improved with a new top surface, I think there was some financial assistance from a brewery.

I recall a time when there was a selection of photographs on display on a table in the clubhouse and a person studying them from the wrong side of the table. I commented to him on how he could possibly make sense of them all upside down. It transpired he was a police photographer at that time (1962) and visited on a number of occasions.

Some of the drivers involved with the Go-Karting were: Eddie Orton who owned a garage in Halifax; Steve Allen who was a partner in another Halifax garage business, Allen and Clark; Alan Lawn, who with his family owned the Bradford Armature Winding Company; John Cotton, son of the John Cotton mill owners at Mirfield; Barry Maskill, a star rider, who went on to run a racing school for budding F1 racers; Tony Dean; Alan Parks, his family had an off-licence at Northowram; Derek Ward, fish shop owner from Wibsey; Tommy Wood, our president and a haulage contractor from Mill Lane in Bradford.

Our fortnightly Sunday afternoon race days were usually attended by approximately 1,000 spectators depending on the weather conditions. The owner, Bert Myers, tried to make it a weekly event as he enjoyed the income through the gate.

As we raced under RAC rules we had to have an RAC driving licence – we also had a Dr Minocha present and members of the St John's Ambulance Brigade for those occasions when there was an accident. All that was over forty years ago. Since those days I have lost contact with the other lads and my interests have moved on to something far less hazardous – barbershop singing.
Laurie Morgan – Bradford (recorded memory September 2006)

Above, left and below: Go-Kart racing at Sunny Vale, *c.* 1963. Helping to create the sense of excitement for the spectators was Robert Brett, the track-side commentator who still lives in the local area and he too has many happy memories of those days. Some of those young men who would almost fly round the track included: Richard Steele, David Cawthra, George Silverwood, Gordon Watkins, David Bryant, Tony Steele (club treasurer) and George Helliwell. The all-important officials who helped to run the meetings included: Harry, Pit Marshal, Roy Allen (clerk of the course), Mr B.F. Beaumont (club chairman), Mrs M.D. Smith (club secretary) and Richard Banks (club press secretary). As many as twenty-five drivers would take part in the race meetings and hundreds of spectators would come to watch the karts reach up speeds of 80mph.

The identities of these Go-Kart racers displaying the numbers 247 and 88 remain a mystery and although there is no date on the photograph, the pudding basin-style crash helmet of number 88 certainly gives a big clue; it is during the early 1960s. Perhaps you are one of these racers or you recognise one of your relatives? I would be very pleased to hear from you if it is someone you know. With each lap measuring a quarter of a mile in length, an eight-lap race took little more than three minutes.

All competitors at Go-Kart race meetings had to have an RAC Kart competition licence and that was compulsory. All the meetings were held under RAC rules and conditions which were designed for safety. If the RAC steward present was not satisfied, he had the authority to stop the race and even the whole meeting if he thought it necessary. With thanks to Laurie Morgan we can look back at the kind of licence that all the

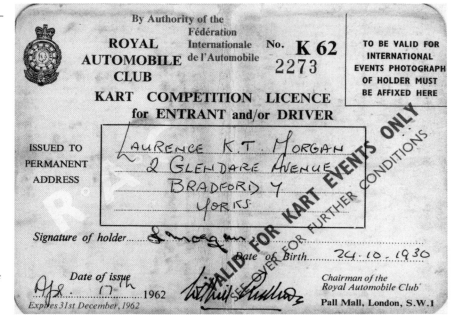

Sunny Vale racers had to have before they were allowed to take part. This was a male–dominated sport and whilst female drivers were welcome under the rules there were no female drivers at Sunny Vale.

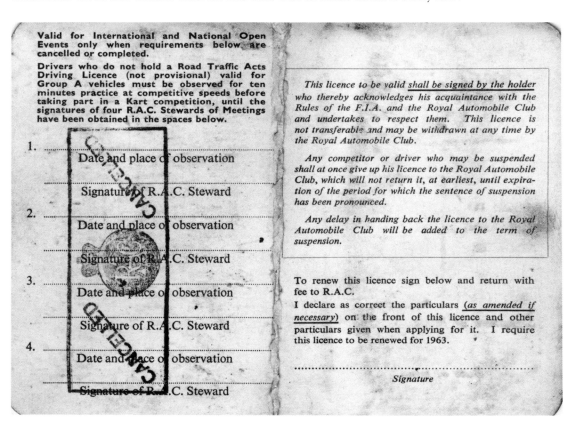

For over thirty years Robert Brett was a visitor to Sunny Vale, firstly as a child and then as race commentator for both the Go-Karts and Stock Car race meetings. He was in the unique position of witnessing first-hand many of the changes from the early post-war period to the final days of the Stock Car era in the early 1980s.

Bales of straw for crash barriers

My earliest memory of visiting Sunny Vale was as a child between 1945 and 1950. On a Bank Holiday mum and dad usually found something special to do and I can remember what would have been my first visit to Sunny Vale. I recall walking down a steep cobbled hill from Hipperholme, then walking on a narrow lane through the valley. I distinctly remember the further we walked, the numbers of pedestrians became a throng, as if a football match was just about to start.

As I got older and eventually attained the ripe old age of a teenager I revisited Sunny Vale – I had a date with a Hipperholme girl. Trying to come up with somewhere different to take her I took her to one or two of the Go-Kart meetings. We both found it difficult to understand what was going on because they did not have a sound system. One of my first jobs was working for Mulland's Electronics and I was spending some time working with 'newfangled' transistor low voltage amplifiers. These were prototypes that had to be tested in the field. I offered to supply a basic PA system to the Go-Kart owners in return for free admission – a deal was struck. Little by little I became more competent as the race-day commentator, until one day I was given the job on a full-time basis.

In the early days the track was unsurfaced but was later given a tarmac surface. The split level track with steep tight bends was a departure from the usual flat circuits and created very exciting races. The club adhered to all the rules and procedures with standard flags for marshals and start and finish staff. There was always a good crowd. There were no crash barriers, just the odd few bales of straw on the tight bends. With the Go-Karts' low ground clearance and low centre of gravity the bales were effective even on the occasions they caught fire. Prizes were awarded at the end of each meeting and at the end of the season.

Lap scoring in the early days was done from parked cars but with this proving to be unsatisfactory a two-storey hut was built. To generate extra revenue during the meeting, interval promotional items were sold to spectators. In 1965 and now living in Lightcliffe, my eldest daughter responded to the local revival of roller-skating. Sunny Vale also responded by reopening the battered old outside roller-skating rink. Now having the opportunity of exploring the gardens I once knew as a child, it was depressing. Most of the original buildings had been wooden except the tea rooms. Near the roller-skating ring was a dilapidated building with some old slot machines in. I also saw the remains of some of the old rides and even parts of the old privet hedge Maze were clearly visible.

The Go-Kart track had not readily impacted too much on the layout of the original gardens but Stock Cars needed a much larger area. It was decided to fill in one of the two lakes (the old rowing boat lake).

In general, Stock Car racing at other venues (Belle Vue etc) had become sophisticated and expensive, so the cheaper Banger racing was introduced. The only requirements were to have a new petrol tank (drivers often used an old fire extinguisher), a crude anti-roll bar and all the windows taken out. As the circuit was not tarmacked, there were no regulations about engine sizes. So when the smaller minis with front-wheel drive were put up against the big Jaguar cars which had poor traction on this surface the races were very exciting. Over a period of time two classes were introduced – Bangers and then the more improved custom-built units but not the F1 Stock Cars standard. The general social activities continued as before, with the drivers' meetings. Disco nights on both Friday and Saturday were very busy and with Wednesday becoming what was called Stag Night, I was kept busy as the club DJ and as in the Go-Kart era many of the Stock Car drivers made Sunny Vale their local.

Robert recalls the occasions when he made a microphone for the purpose of a pit-side interview with a driver – this concept was unheard of at a local meeting. However, these interviews did not last long because of the 'fruity' language of the drivers echoing throughout the valley and not something for the ears of younger spectators.

Unlike Go-Karts, Stock Cars was a contact sport and the so-called Banger races often left the track littered with bits of cars, none more so than on the demolition derby races when it was absolute mayhem for anything up to three quarters of an hour, when the whole idea was to be the last car standing.

The success of Stock Car racing at Sunny Vale lasted until the 1980s. Another new track had opened at Odsal Stadium and drivers were drawn away from Sunny Vale to the new track and as the Stock Car drivers moved on so did the spectators.

In his early days at Sunny Vale, Robert took a small cutting from a magenta rhododendron for the garden of his new house at Lightcliffe. What is now a huge shrub in his garden always blossoms around the start of the Go-Kart and Stock Car seasons and is a constant reminder of those happy years he spent down in the valley.

In 1958 after Bert Myers had bought Sunny Vale he said to the press that 'Sunny Vale is a challenge… in previous years it has been a challenge to so many men with similar visions as I have, but always the three evils of decay, vandalism and industrial grime were not far away'. The halcyon days remembered by so many had now gone, but would they ever return?

In 1972 the Sunny Vale Country Club was sold by Bert Myers and his wife and a new team from Kingston-upon-Thames took over, Albert and Ellen Gale, who, in partnership with their daughter Rita and husband Gaston Delorme, bought Sunny Vale with a high expectation of success.

This is the front cover of a Stock Car programme from the late 1960s and the only one I know to have survived from the Bert Myers era at Sunny Vale.

It was in 1972 that an advertisement appeared in the *Surrey Comet* describing what sounded to be an idyllic property sale, 'the Sunny Vale Pleasure Gardens' near Halifax, West Yorkshire. Rita immediately fell in love with the idea of moving to Yorkshire, 'sounds fantastic'. Rita's father Albert was looking to take things a little easier owing to his ill health, but Ellen, her mother, didn't like the idea at all.

They decided to take a look out of interest, and arrived at Sunny Vale on a Stock Car day. Driving down what was a rickety old road in a distinctive bright yellow Pontiac motor car, everyone, except Rita, was for turning round and going back home.

Even Rita was beginning to be turned off the idea, 'just looking at the dirty children was enough to want to go back home', she thought. It was only later that she discovered they were dirty because of the ash dust from the Stock Car races. There were no concrete paths; everywhere they looked there was mud and lots of it.

Sunny Vale Promotions

Stock Car Racing

THRILLS & SPILLS

2.30 p.m.

ADMITTANCE TO SUNNY VALE GARDENS

Car No.	Name	Car No.	Name	Car No.	Name
1	LEN TODD	138	MIKE COWELL	379	DAVE MITCHELL
2	GRAHAM SHARPE	142	DAVE SHAW	384	ROY MARSDEN
3	BUTTY HAYHURST	143	DEREK BOWLES	389	DAVE BULL
4	BRIAN BRANSON	148	BOB CHEW	390	JACK BARRACLOUGH
5	DAVE BEVERLEY	151	KEITH GOMERSALL	396	JOHN PULLAN
6	JOHN SAINT	154	GEORGE SPENCER	398	PHILLIP HAYHURST
7	V. MURAMAA	155	TONY HUDSON	399	ALAN JENNINGS
11	MAC SMITH	160	BILL CUNNINGHAM	400	JOHN DIXON
12	BRIAN LANA	161	TONY HEATHCOTE	401	PHIL HART
18	PAUL MARTIN	163	JOHN WILLIAMS	402	ROGER SNOWDEN
19	PETER DAVIS	165	MARY AKROYD	403	FRANK PHILIPS
21	SUSAN GENTLE	166	TED HORSLEY	404	DAVE TETLEY
22	ALLEN HIGGINS	175	PHILIP HORSFALL	405	BRIAN HOOPER
23	DAVID ROWLAND	180	FRANK PILKINGTON	406	FRANK BATTY
24	NIGEL GENTLE	181	KEN HUDSON	407	JOHN ROBERTS
25	PAULINE HIGGINS	183	STUART McKIE	408	TREVOR KIRKHAM
27	KEN SMALES	189	JOHN DAVIS	409	HOWARD LEAROYD
31	GORDON ROSS	191	TERRY DAVIS	410	IAN BARKER
34	SUSAN HOMAN	195	RODEN VARLEY	411	COLIN CRAVEN
35	IRVINE HOMAN	196	ROY SPENCER	412	LES EVANS
36	CHUCK HORSFIELD	203	COLIN POXON	413	DEREK EVANS
37	JOHN WRIGLEY	206	NORMAN HANDLEY	414	HAROLD BLACKBURN
40	FRANK AKROYD	207	CHARLES CAMPBELL	415	GEOFF PILKINGTON
41	TOM AKROYD	208	KEN LONG	416	PAUL CAVE
42	PETE CORY	209	PAUL BLACKWELL	417	PETE SMITH
43	BRIAN SANDERSON	211	TONY McGRATH	418	ANDY RITCHIE
44	KEN JONES	212	JOHN CHANDLER	419	PETE BLAKE
45	ALAN SMITH	214	RON SAYLES	420	ROGER CREEK
46	LEN KNAPTON	215	DES BURKE	421	DAVE McCANN
48	ROY HODGSON	225	GEORGE HANNAH	422	ALAN JOHNSON
49	JEFF WAKEFIELD	226	IAN THOMPSON	423	TONY STUBBS
51	RODNEY SHEARD	228	DOODY HAYHURST	424	PETER BOULD
52	GRAHAM GERRARD	231	NIGEL FAIRCLOUGH	425	KEITH JUBB
53	DAVE RANFIELD	239	MIKE LAWRENCE	426	MALC COLINS
57	PHIL LOVE	243	ED HILES	427	BRIAN VASEY
58	BRIAN HARPER	246	MALCOLM BRIGGS	428	MIKE SELLERS
59	ALAN LLOYD	247	JOE ASKHAM	429	ROY JOHNSON
60	ALAN BOOTH	252	JACK HAIGH	430	FRANK THORNTON
61	BOB WOOLER	258	DAVE FERRIDGE	431	ERNEST THORNTON
65	MAC GREEN	259	VIC HEDGES	432	LESLIE THORNTON
66	BRIAN LEECH	260	ROY PAGE	433	ERIC THORNTON
68	GERALD STUBBS	261	KEITH MARSHALL	434	TERRY THORNTON
69	TONY KIRKNESS	262	ALLAN FORREST	435	ALF TURTON
70	ALF HART	265	DAVE SIMMS	436	FRANK STEEL
72	JOHN AKROYD	273	FRED NOTHERS	437	TONY HANSELL
73	DAVE CARTER	274	KEN WARRINER	438	FRED SMITH
74	BRIAN TAYLOR	276	GRAHAM MARSHALL	439	BRIAN VOSE
81	RICHARD ROPER	284	DAVE TOWNEND	440	STEPHEN ROUNDHILL
89	GEORGE BOYLES	286	BRIAN SCARR	441	BRIAN NORTON
90	MIKE SHAW	287	JOHN WHITEHURST	442	RON MALLION
91	STEVE HOPKINSON	288	COLIN GAUTRY	443	FRANK BOSTOCK
92	TED BRANSON	295	ALAN WILCOCK	444	DALE METCALFE
94	JOHN HOPKINSON	311	PHIL SMITH	445	MAX JUMEAUX
99	DENNIS HOLDSWORTH	315	CHRIS GREED		
101	HAROLD DAVIS	317	TERRY CALLAGHAN		
102	MIKE ROBINSON	320	JOHN DUCKWORTH		
108	BARRY HAIGH	324	DAVE WILKINSON		
109	KEITH NESTOR	326	TOM WILKINSON		
110	BRIAN YOUNG	329	GORDON PARKIN		
112	STEVE TETLEY	330	ERIC DAWSON		
115	BILL CUMMINGS	331	NELSON HAYHURST		
116	GRAHAM HALL	345	BOB FORREST		
117	BERT PAYNE	346	JOHN IRWIN		
118	OLIVER METCALFE	348	BOB SNOWDEN		
119	ARTHUR METCALFE	349	KEITH PETTY		
128	GRAHAM RUTTER	352	PHIL RAWNSLEY		
129	RAY IRVING	364	BERNARD BALDWIN		
131	GARTH JACKSON	366	RICH SUGDEN		
133	MEL HOLLINGWORTH	367	ALAN HARRIS		
134	DEREK HIRST	371	ALAN SCOTT		
135	ANT HIRST	372	NIEL HARLAND		
136	MIKE WEBSTER	373	MIKE SPEIGHT		

Left: A list of drivers and their race numbers for the season.

Mr Myers, the owner, went to meet them and showed them round the whole site. He took them to see the three cottages that went with the sale, along with the clubhouse. Rita loved it and was keen to persuade her parents and husband Gaston (Gab) that it would be a good move. Their return trip was in September, on a glorious sunny day. That was it, they were now all hooked and the sale went through in December 1972. In 1973 they reopened the club and life at Sunny Vale was once again springing into life.

Once the club had re-established itself, the Stock Car racing was restarted in October 1973 and was initially very successful. This is the back page of the programme and lists Robert Brett as the commentator, a position he held until Stock Racing ended at Sunny Vale in 1980.

The prize money never actually left the clubhouse

I think there were about a dozen of us who were considered as regular drivers who would race every other weekend but there were about 150 registered drivers and usually around fifty, maybe as many as sixty would turn up, this included both Stock Cars and Bombers (Bangers). The teams used to bring their own supporters – family and friends. The awards and prize money used to be distributed on Tuesday nights after the racing, so you will appreciate just how and why the prize money never actually left the clubhouse...
Paul Williams – Florida, USA (recorded memory March 2006)

Number 20, *c.* 1978, the distinctive Rover, owned by one of Sunny Vale's regular Stock Car drivers, Brian Fox aka 'Sly One'. Sitting on top and surveying the carnage is Dean Ramsden. Looking at the minimal damage sustained by Brian's car, this might have been one of his better race days.

One of the top Stock Car drivers at Sunny Vale and regarded as the one to beat was number 77 driven by Bonnar Coleano. Although his mini looks as though it is on its last legs, judging from him waving the victory flag it was another good day for him. Bonnar also wrote editorial for the fan magazine, under the pen name of 'Rannob'.

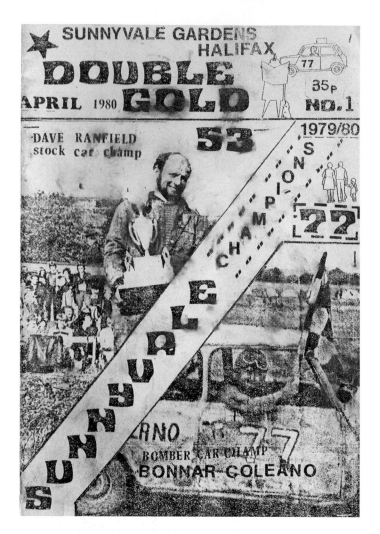

Sunny Vale racing fans

We used to be dedicated Sunny Vale racing fans. In fact Bonnar Coleano, my daughter and I started a newsletter fan magazine. We only produced three issues before the news came that Sunny Vale was shutting down. The magazine proved to be so popular and sold that well I have only got one copy of the first issue left now.

Some of the other racing drivers I can remember from those days were Dean and Jack Gill, Andy French, Stan Boulton, Ken Hopes and Ian Smith. With Ken Hopes, Ian Smith and Bonnar Coleano all going into BriSCA F1 (British Stock Car Association), some of the other drivers went racing at Brampton. In fact Dean Gill was still racing there the last I heard.
Jean Vasey (recorded memory March 2006)

Opposite above: The Sunny Vale Stock Car drivers had another side to their characters and that was fundraising, particularly for the St John's Ambulance Brigade. St John's would have some representatives at all the Sunny Vale Stock Car meetings ready to deal with any incident where someone at the meeting needed medical assistance.

Sunny Vale Pram Push

We went and did a Pram Push
To Sowerby Bridge from Sunny
We called in pubs along the way
It was really quite funny

The locals they all laughed at us
And Keith in his wife's old knickers
Shook the bucket in their faces
Ignoring laughs and titters

We had to push some people
To get them out of town
Or we wouldn't get to St John's
Before the light went down
We raised a lot of money

And gave it to St John's
So they could buy an ambulance
To carry patients on
St John's are our real heroes
They spend their own free time
So I can feel real safe
Whilst I'm enjoying mine

A happy day was had by all

Following the decision that the Stock Car meetings would end in 1980, permission was granted in 1982 to use the track as a landfill site. Whilst there was disappointment from many of the drivers, Stock Car racing as a major spectator event at Sunny Vale had been gradually coming to a natural end.

This scene is looking across the corner of the Stock Car track towards the top lake – where all the cars are parked in the distance was where all the activities were centred in the early days of Sunny Vale's amusement park.

Before the landfill site could begin, all the tyres had to be removed from the site. Although the Stock Car era had now come to an end the clubhouse was still doing well and new opportunities were on the horizon.

Over 1,000 tyres were removed from the site – the pile of tyres in this picture marks where the top end of the old Victoria Lake used to be. Behind the line of trees behind the tyres is the lane that leads down to Pinnell Bridge where you could then turn right onto the public footpath. This would eventually bring you out at the back of the Maze, a familiar route to all those children who visited before the Boer War and both the First and Second World Wars.

Sticking out from the building line of the old tea rooms and now the clubhouse is the Webster's Brewery sign. During the 1970s squash was becoming a very popular sport but in the Calderdale area (with the exception of the one in Halifax) squash clubs were in short supply. Having developed the public bar and dance hall in 1977 they built a series of squash courts. In the summer of 1978 the Sunny Vale squash club opened and it was soon able to have both a men's and ladies' team, as well as individual players. For the first time in many years Sunny Vale was doing well and proving to be successful. In the wooden structure on the left-hand side rumours have circulated for many years that the Sunny Vale monkeys were supposed to have been housed in this building. To date I have found no evidence to support they ever existed and the story remains but a myth.

Left: The Sunny Vale squash club ladies' first team, *c.* 1984. The members are, back row, from left to right: Hazel Sanderson and Gillian Robinson. Front row: Pauline Heal, Linda Littlefair and Sandra Delorme.

Opposite above: In July 1983 disaster struck when a fire devastated the clubhouse. At the time of the fire Gab and Rita were away on holiday and it was left to Albert, Ellen and their son to try and sort it all out. The club had closed as usual that night and following the clearing away and then locking up at 3 a.m., everything at that time seemed fine. First news of the fire came from a neighbour who rang them at 6.45 a.m. to say they could see the fire from across the valley. Whilst they managed to salvage some motorcycles as well as saving their two dogs and some chickens, everything else was lost. The final cost was ten years of hard work which had all gone up in smoke in less than ten minutes – the financial loss was estimated at £80,000.

Opposite below: In the winter of 1987 there was an opportunity that the Alexandra Lake area might once again come to life with the Manpower Service Commission in conjunction with the United Reformed Church Charities using a grant to do some much-needed restoration work.

With the restoration work well under way, the Alexandra Lake was soon beginning to look nice again. Some of the many visitors who came down to Sunny Vale at this time on their own personal nostalgia trips were heard to comment that the lake was beginning to look a bit like the old days.

It was on this track where the 'Baby Bunce' miniature railway ran. Some of the workers at the site told me they even found some of the old railway track sleepers. Work continued into the summer of 1988 and I remember visiting the site in May of that year and recall being very impressed with the work that had been done.

Small seating areas were created. Perhaps once the lake was finished picnics would once again be the order of the day. Sadly it was not to be – even the new picnic seats were stolen.

One of the hardest jobs was to clear away the years of debris and neglect, rebuilding the walls and getting the water moving again. The lake had become a huge stagnant pond, but once the overflow channels were cleared and this huge channel on the left which ran alongside the full length of the lake was unblocked life was slowly coming back again to this forgotten area.

Unfortunately, once the initial grant had run out, the work to renovate the lake came to any end. This photograph shows the Alexandra Lake in May 1988. Sadly since this work came to an end the site has almost returned to the state it was in before the work began. 'A waste of money': without a doubt it was. If the work could have continued being financed who knows what we might have been seeing on the lake today.

From 1984 the Sunny Vale skip hire company was a busy aspect of the work at Sunny Vale and kept going until Gaston (Gab) Delorme retired in 2003. The landfill tipping finally came to an end in the early 1990s.

The squash club closed in 1995. When it opened it was one of the few clubs in West Yorkshire and became very popular. However, as the sport had taken off and its popularity had grown, even more clubs had opened and Sunny Vale found that their squash club was not a viable business anymore.

From the ashes of the fire in the summer of 1983 the clubhouse did rise again. Today many local people will, I am sure, remember using the club facility for their family function or works 'Christmas do', or even wedding reception. The catering side of the business was very popular.

The clubhouse stayed open another year but it was not long before it had its own problems and in 1996, after Gab and his family celebrated his birthday, it too closed its doors for the last time.

Since that date the old squash club has been converted in to three private dwellings; a project that was completed in 2003. Development work has continued with George Watson, a local builder working on more of the old cottage buildings.

This local building company is based in Station Road and occupies the old Hipperholme Railway Station site, a station that closed on the 6 June 1953. In its heyday this station witnessed literally tens of thousands of visitors to Sunny Vale, visitors who had travelled from all over the North of England.

ten

Gone, But
Not Forgotten

Over the years, many people have taken the time to share their memories with me. Occasionally they will give or loan me picture postcards or small pieces of memorabilia. This small box which was given to me many years ago contains a pair of pink table napkin rings made from styrene. Written on the box are the words, 'Sunny Vale' and the owner has written on the year, 1922. It was the type of gift or prize available from one of the sideshows at Sunny Vale.

Having got to know the present owners of the Sunny Vale site, Gaston (Gab) and Rita Delorme, they have over the years unearthed a number of items from the old days, which they have kindly made available for this publication. The obverse of this piece shows a picture of the large lake with the words, 'Sunny Vale Pleasure Gardens, Hipperholme' underneath, whilst on the reverse side is a mirror.

This is the kind of thing a small child would have won, perhaps on their Annual Sunday School Treat excursion to Sunny Vale and would then have proudly shown off to their parents once they returned home again.

Above left: Quite often at collectors' fairs, bottles bearing the name 'Ganson of Hove Edge' will be on sale. Shown here is an old Codd bottle. It is said to have been Hiram Codd, a salesman from a cork company, who patented the first bottle that had a glass marble in the neck in 1872. It was the Codd bottle which gave its name to that well-known English phrase, 'coddswallop'. Just how old this Ganson's codd bottle is, is difficult to say.

Above right: Another Ganson's bottle, only this one has a screw top – date unknown.

Another Ganson's bottle in close up, showing the company name on the glass – date unknown. Ganson's, throughout their history, would have sold tens of thousands of bottles to Sunny Vale visitors. But with the amount of excavation work both for racing and tipping purposes at Sunny Vale it is highly unlikely that any bottles have survived.

Above and below: I made a nostalgic visit to Sunny Vale in the summer of 1990 and as I walked past what were the old tea rooms I came across this rotting dilapidated building (also see page 111). Hidden away inside was this pay booth, whilst the most noticeable thing was the graffiti painted on the wooden flap. But as I looked at the top lintel I could just about make out the faded words, 'keep this side clear of cycles'. Sadly even the old dilapidated building with the pay booth has now gone.

A point which is often raised about Sunny Vale is whether they had any animals or not. From all my research I have found no evidence that they kept any animals other than donkeys and ponies. However, there is a long-held rumour that there were once some monkeys kept on the site. It has even been suggested that they were housed in the building shown above – but I have my doubts.

It is likely that the rumours about animals being kept probably date back to the days of the old Halifax Zoo (1909-1916) at Chevinedge at Exley (between Elland and Sidall near Halifax) and the story of animals actually refers to the animals they used to have.

Above: This was a scene in the summer of 1990 when Edward Helme, then aged nine, was captured looking through the pay hatch hoping to pay his entrance money. This building was the last vestige of the old Stock Car days. 'Sorry son, it's closed. If you wanted the amusement park you are over fifty years too late or was it the Go-Karts or was it the Stock Car racing? For those you are just over thirty years to late,' commented a passer-by.

Right: This was the last advertisement sign at Sunny Vale Gardens.

William and Susannah Henley

On Sunday 26 November 1939 William died at Halifax General Hospital. He was a resident of South Lynn Cottage, Sunny Vale, Hipperholme and eighty years of age. He was a native of Gloucestershire and came to Hipperholme in the 1880s and with Joseph Bunce he helped to construct Sunny Vale. He helped to plant the original Maze, which was remodelled and enlarged in 1907. Prior to that he had been a carrier and also drove a coach from Gloucester to Stroud and other places. The continual applications by Sunday schools to hold picnics in the fields led to the idea of constructing the pleasure grounds. He was of great assistance to Mr Bunce when the project began in 1881. Between them they constructed the boating lakes and arranged the layout of the grounds. For a long period of time he was Mr Bunce's right-hand man and in later years took over the running of the boats and when it was possible to skate on the water. He worked at Sunny Vale until he was seventy-five years old. He was in excellent health up until his untimely death and was a lifelong teetotaller and a founder member of the Welcome Tent Hipperholme in the Rechobites movement. He lost his eldest and youngest sons in the First World War.

Tommy Womersley

Womersley was the Horse Keeper but looked after the animals generally. They had eight to ten donkeys and then there were Oxo and Bovril, the two Shetland ponies.

Harry Rothery and Harold Brier

These two men were responsible for the roller-skating.

Dick Cracknell

He followed on after Fred and Ivy as the caretaker, c. 1946.

Tommy Morris

Hall of Mirrors.

Fred and Ivy King

This couple lived in the grounds as caretakers and generally Fred

was the one to chase the kids out. He also looked after Kitty the carthorse

Annie Morris

This lady worked in the tea rooms during the 1930s.

Mrs Ripley

She was the wife of Fred Ripley who owned the ice-cream business at the junction of Sutcliffe Wood Bottom Lane and Half House Lane. She worked on their ice-cream stall in the grounds of Sunny Vale

Nellie Brown

She ran one of the stalls.

Ada Risely

She was the manageress of the tea rooms.

Mrs Coleman

She was a waitress in the tea rooms.

John and his wife (no details of their surname)

He was the joiner but they also kept the Automatic Café stocked up for customers.

Willie Kershaw

He was in charge of the boat rides on the big lake. He left to join the services in 1939.

...and finally...

With such wonderful people all aiming to ensure you had such a good time, what better way to finish to off the day than calling on your way home at Willie Chadwick's fish shop for 'a fish and a pen 'orth' at the end of Half House Lane? Those were the days.

Lasting Memories

During its heyday Sunny Vale employed scores of ladies from the community who went to work both full-time and part-time in the tea rooms, making ham and tongue sandwiches in the unique Sunny Vale way. Many readers will be aware there has always been an unwritten rank structure within tea room circles. You just try and take a job on that Mrs 'so and so' had done for years and you are taking your life into your own hands.

It was often said that you could tell who had 'done sandwiches' before down at Sunny Bunces, particularly because of the tea-room supervisor Ada Risely, who ran the tea room like a well-oiled machine and ruled it with a rod of iron…

The matrons who prowled round the local chapel bazaar tea tables would often be seen lifting the edges of sandwiches for inspection before the masses were allowed to pour in to their temporary tea room. They would be often heard to comment to each other in soft whispering voices, 'Mrs so and so, does a nice sandwich, she worked at Bunces you know' – a real qualification in itself.

My abiding memory is of the meal

In 1953 I was teaching in St Patrick's Infant School, Bradford. That year the church celebrated the centenary of its opening and it was decided that all the school children would be taken to Sunny Vale as a treat. At that time there were three separate schools, each with a headmistress (all three were nuns then of course). The infant-cum-nursery school where the children were from three to seven years old was then very large because at that time we had what was known as the post-war bulge, that is the children born when the men returned from the war.

From the age of seven the boys and girls moved to separate schools and there they stayed until they left at fifteen, apart from the few who passed the eleven-plus exam and moved on. All three schools also had a large influx of Polish and Ukrainian children so altogether there must have been more than 600 children. I well remember that throughout the fifties and early sixties there were between forty-five and fifty children in every class.

On the appointed day we all walked from Westgate to the railway station and, as you can imagine, we almost brought the city to a standstill. A special train had been booked but we discovered it had no corridor so we had to enlist some of the senior girls to sit in with the younger children. However, we arrived safely and the children had a wonderful time. I don't recall many details but oddly enough I do remember the song that was blaring out from the loudspeaker as we approached; it was a popular song of the day called 'Give Me Five Minutes More'. We had just the one mishap with only one girl falling into the lake, so that was not too bad.

My abiding memory is of the meal. We had been sent a menu beforehand and the meal had been booked and because of the numbers we had to go into the café in relays so the infants went in first. After they had eaten their sandwiches and sausage rolls etc, we waited and waited but nothing else was forthcoming so eventually the head asked about the fruit and custard which had been ordered. The answer was, 'it won't be long Sister' and that someone had just gone into the garden to cut the rhubarb. Well you can imagine the Sister's reaction – she was furious while the rest of the staff were trying to stifle their laughter and all the older children were waiting outside for their meal. We often laughed about it later.

In the end we got them all safely back to Bradford – the station platform was packed with parents who were all anxiously waiting for their offspring. A memorable day indeed!
Miss Hilda Bolton – Stowmarket, Suffolk (recorded memory August 2006)

Singing about 'Holidays at Home'

During the war Percy Bunce J.P. became Mayor of Brighouse (1942-1944). He promoted 'Holidays at Home' and we all learned a song about that. I recall singing it with all the other local children around the shelter on Lightcliffe Stray, with Percy present to watch.

It began, 'we'll have a holiday in Brighouse, we'll have a holiday at home'. It went on to relate listening to the Brighouse and Rastrick Band, and also spending holiday time at Sunny Vale. For some celebration or other, all the school children in the borough were given vouchers to spend on the amusements at Sunny Vale. On one occasion Percy Bunce even had posters about Sunny Vale stuck up and displayed in Blackpool. I was told that for the Silver Jubilee of 1935 the Bunce family gave away lots of free tickets.

Don Thompson – Wheaton Aston, Stafford (recorded memory August 2006)

From the top of Red Moor a wonderful panorama lay at our feet

As a little girl during the war years I lived with my parents near the Travellers inn at Hipperholme. I remember the crowds of people pouring over the old railway bridge and down the hill into Sunny Vale. Trains carried visitors from all over Yorkshire and rows of double-decker buses were to be seen at weekends lined up outside the 'Travs' and along Halifax Old Road and up by the Old Dumb Mill (this was also a public house which was opened in the nineteenth century but closed during the mid-1940s).

At the top of the hill a one-legged man sat on the ground turning the handle of a hurdy-gurdy box. The strains of 'Little Sir Echo' resounded round the area, driving locals mad but providing an entertainment for the crowds, who also threw him money. Over the tops of the rocky hill, we children played in fear of an elderly man who seemed to haunt the quarries (now all filled in of course) nearby. We knew him as 'Puffty Bill' and from a safe distance we taunted him shouting, 'Puffty Bill, swallowed a pill twice as big as Beacon Hill'. On reflection I believe him to have been guarding explosives used in quarry blasting at that time.

From the top of the hill, known locally as the Red Moor – a wonderful panorama of the Walterclough Valley and Sunny Vale – lay at our feet, and the boats on the two lakes could be clearly seen.

We would run down the hill, through the oak trees, across the lane and down again into the daisy field. From here access to Sunny Vale could be obtained via a pipe across the Red Beck. Further round, along a muddy path overhung with trees, another way in (without paying of course) could be found at the back of the Maze. My father, a soldier at that time, was a member of a sick club at Halifax. Children of members were given a trip to Sunny Vale each year. We were issued with a variety of coloured tickets which admitted us to the amusements, boats, concerts and tea. Matinées for the concert were given in the afternoon and evening. We sat out in all weathers often getting soaked. Suddenly a figure would appear at the side shouting, 'Halifax Sick Club, tea's ready'. A mad scramble followed as adults and children dashed up the slope to the tea rooms where long tables covered with potted-meat sandwiches and buns were to be found, 'I didn't like it'.

There were many amusements but I remember the Maze, donkeys, skating rink, Hall of Mirrors, boating lakes and the Helter-Skelter. Halfway down the Helter-Skelter there was a little ridge in the metal which precipitated the occupant of the mat a few inches into the air and down the remaining half of the slide with a whoosh, into the arms of men waiting at the bottom to catch people. It this wasn't done well, then legs scraped along very hairy mats and were left smarting for hours.

On the approach to Sunny Vale, many Polish soldiers were often to be seen returning from work at Allen's brickyard which was situated nearby. There were also soldiers residing at Shibden Barracks, which was formerly a remand home for boys. Lorry loads of soldiers were regularly seen down Tan House Hill and along Halifax Old Road. Many soldiers mingled with the crowds at Sunny Vale, spending their leisure hours there. In 1947 the lakes were frozen and many people came to skate on the little lake. It was truly a winter wonderland. We children were allowed to slide on the ice. After the thaw the nearby 'Red Beck' became a swollen torrent as it threaded its way through the valley.

Mrs Lily Dobson, née Chippendale – Wyke, Bradford (recorded memory February 1991)

It was magic and I've never forgotten it

My family lived in Bradford in the 1930s, in the days before the NHS when most people joined a Benefit Society to cover their healthcare. My father joined the Ancient Order of Foresters and because he was a member we three children qualified for an annual Christmas party and also for the summer outing. This was often to Sunny Vale Gardens because it was such a popular place.

Just before the summer outing the Foresters sent our tickets and a green enamelled Foresters Badge with a bow and arrow insignia on it.

We all assembled at Laisterdyke Railway Station in Bradford, all agog. We had strict instructions, 'get back away from the platform edge'. I can see the engine now, all steam and smoke and of course soot. I cannot remember where our destination station was; perhaps it was Hipperholme because we didn't walk very far. We approached Sunny Vale via a steep cobbled cutting and there it was!

The lakes, the boats and all the amusements – to someone who was just seven years old it was a vast place. Despite the years two things are clear: a Helter-Skelter, which I loved and the café where they had something I had never seen before, nor since, a row of faucets, like squat ornamental taps set in the wall. You put coppers in the slot of your choice and out spewed a measure of pop, lemonade or orangeade or even dandelion and burdock. It was magic and I've never forgotten it. It's all so vague now. I think we had tokens or tickets as money, again from the Foresters.

About fifteen years ago I was visiting my family in Mirfield and we were driving around and I saw a sign saying 'Hipperholme'. We stopped and asked where Sunny Vale Gardens used to be. The people had no idea – how sad, it was Yorkshire's answer to Las Vegas!

Irene Hedges née Sewell – Worthing (recorded memory July 2006)

Well, there you have it – Sunny Bunces. Yes, I am sure some readers will say, 'but what about so and so' or 'you have not mentioned the man who looked after the, you know'. Over the last twenty years I have given slide presentations about Sunny Vale the length and breadth of the county and whether it was in Doncaster or Leyburn I am always asked why it came to an end.

Sunny Vale had what I call its time slot in history, just as Belle Vue did in Manchester and all those other smaller parks you can remember from your childhood days. 'Well, why can't those days come back again?' That is another question I am often asked. Well, through these pages you have all seen the layout of the picturesque but small Walterclough Valley. I would ask you a question, 'where would you park over 100 coaches or 500 motor cars at the summer peak visiting times?' The valley would come to a standstill and neither the existing road, which is the same road in as it is out again, nor of course the neighbours, could cope with such a massive intrusion.

I have met many people who still remember those halcyon days of yesteryear, the days when almost everyone walked down into the valley unhindered and with barely a care in the world. Taking a last look at the Lilywhite's postcard on the previous page, although the Central Park Railway Station (top left) has long since gone, do not forget the train today can be seen in the National Railway Museum at York. The amusement arcade building and the bandstand (top right) have also long since gone but the maple dance floor which was originally laid in 1909 is still in use today. It was taken to an engineering company in Bradford where I understand it still is.

The Victoria Lake (bottom left) is but a distant memory and whilst few can recall the winter skating sessions of yesteryear many do remember when it was used by the Stock Car drivers and then as a landfill site. The landfill work ceased many years ago and the site is now but a haven for the local wildlife.

The larger Alexandra Lake (bottom right) is still there but whilst half is overgrown with water weeds, the water is still there; the other half of the lake can clearly be seen. Looking at it today it is difficult to imagine the launch or as the pre-First World War youngsters referred to it, a 'ship'; or the one fleeting moment during the 1960s when Dan Rhodes was caught on camera attempting to remove the silt, in anticipation that the planned water skiing was to be the new business venture and a lasting saviour for the old place.

Nothing now remains of those far-off days – except if you look at the rhododendrons and holly bushes that grow all around the site. Seeing these in such abundance you are bound, if only for a fleeting moment think to yourself – now why are these here?

Epilogue

Having spent the last twenty years away from my beloved Yorkshire, I frequently need to return to the scene of my childhood, Sunny Vale. This finds me leaning against a broken fence overlooking the lake, trespassing. Many years ago this was once my playground; it was a field where the blackberries grew in profusion, where my brother Peter and I burnt Guy Fawkes and feasted on spuds. It was where Oxo and Bovril, the two ponies, spent their retirement. They, like the ancient boat resting under the trees, were part of the landscape.

I don't see it as it is now, but remember it as it was, bursting with life. A place humming with children's voices; Baby Bunce, the miniature train, shrieking its way through the black tunnel; clattering roller skates or, in winter, the silence – when the whole valley was covered in a blanket of snow and the swish of ice-skates accompanied by strains of 'The Skaters' Waltz'.

I indulged in its privacy on Sunday mornings; I could take out a boat and converse with Nelly the swan, or rescue delinquent moorhens from the most inept mothers. Other times I would peer into the murky waters of the old lake and watch the millions of tadpoles nestling their velvety heads into its mossy sides. It was where the lone almond tree blossomed; where the bright green crumpled heads of the newly born rhubarb leaves pushed themselves into the world and where soon the masses of rhododendrons would splash their colours. The air resounded with the song of the blackbird and thrush, as Peter and I stood on a carpet of bluebells, sharing chocolate creams and secrets.

At the end of the season, the valley changed its act. The boats and swings were repaired and painted; the Grecian figures were cleaned and packed to sleep away the winter – gruelling work which the visitors never witnessed. Then I would escape to the tack room and sit before a crackling fire, listening to Tommy imparting his words of wisdom. From a man who had spent his life working on the land, it was profound. This sanctuary was a place of mystery, dim and draped in cobwebs, smelling of hay and Kitty the carthorse. Narrow steps clung to the wall, taking anyone brave enough up, up, into a black void. We were forbidden to venture lest we break a leg. Unnecessary threats. Its dark mysteries were sufficient deterrent.

In winter the curtain went up on yet another scene, that of providing holly and the making of wreaths for local schools and shops. There was an invasion of local men and women to join the regular staff. It was a happy time, lots of singing and joking and always the huge black stove to bring back life to freezing fingers.

Throughout the war my older brother, Peter, joined the navy and served on *The Victorious* aircraft carrier. He returned home to find his beloved gardens were to be sold. Sunny Vale ran in his blood. I still have his letters written throughout the war, telling of his plans and the longing to return to the valley so dear to him. This, I am sure, broke his heart. He died on his fiftieth birthday.

How I would love to retrace my steps round what was the old lake. There was magic there. Always was. Where the huge holly trees stood like sentinels, guarding the young pear and apple trees. Always the smell of rich sweet earth and at night the heavens jam-packed with stars.

I seldom think of the amusements, other than the fun house and the distorting mirrors. I don't need distorting mirrors now, life is full of compensations. These days, I may forget what day it is, but ask me to recount memories of Sunny Vale – I dare you! The Valley of the Wild Boar sleeps not. Thanks to Chris Helme, memories will be captured within the pages of his book and I will be eternally grateful. Not mentioning those who are looking down from above and giving a wry smile.

Mrs Lionne Crossley
Granddaughter of the late Joseph Bunce

Other local titles published by Tempus

Brighouse and District
CHRIS HELME

This fascinating collection of over 200 archive photographs illustrates some of the historical developments which have shaped the town and district of Brighouse. The Industrial Revolution and the coming of the Canal Age brought new prosperity to the area, and this book describes the effects of industrialisation on the town and the people who helped to bring it about, as well as the industries themselves. Explore the buildings, transport and shops, as well as the close-knit communities which have formed the heart of the area.

978 0 7524 3577 0

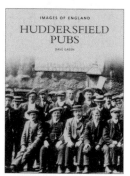

Elland Revisited
BRIAN HARGREAVES

This fascinating collection of more than 200 archive images explores the history and development of Elland and the surrounding district over the last century and records the Elland of a former age. Over the centuries industry has played a vital part, and agriculture, textiles, quarrying and engineering at local, national and international levels have helped to put the town on the map. This book, compiled by the president of the Greater Elland Historical Society, documents both the industrial heritage and everyday life of the area.

978 0 7524 4145 0

Huddersfield Pubs
DAVID GREEN

This book is an illustrated, historical tour of the pubs and beerhouses of Huddersfield and its environs by one of the town's best-known experts on the subject. The author has spent many years collecting old photographs, anecdotes and interesting information about the area's pubs and he draws on these resources and his considerable knowledge to compile this fascinating account, which also includes reference to the many local breweries, past and present, as well as to many of the area's best known pub characters: landlords and customers, famous and infamous!

978 07524 4165 8

Huddersfield Voices
ERROL HANNON

This fascinating collection, containing more than eighty photographs from private collections, is a 'people's history' of Huddersfield. These reminiscences of life in the town over the last century, through periods of war, industrial decline and profound change, evoke a world where the mills were booming, many children picked potatoes during half term and all female teachers had to wear a hat on their way to school.

978 0 7524 3714 9

If you are interested in purchasing other books published by Tempus, or in case you have difficulty finding any Tempus books in your local bookshop, you can also place orders directly through our website

www.tempus-publishing.com